THE GOSPEL
ACCORDING TO
CULTURE

ClearDay

THE GOSPEL ACCORDING TO CULTURE

Published by Clear Day Publishing, a division of Clear Day Media Group LLC, Waco, TX. cleardaypublishing.com.

Published in association with Lux Creative {theluxcreative.com}

ISBN: 978-1-7326252-2-8

Cover Design: Bethany Lo Design {bethanylo.design@gmail.com}
Interior Design: Lux Creative {theluxcreative.com}
Printed in the United States of America.

TABLE OF CONTENTS

INTRODUCTION

A brilliant meteor shot through the sky ahead of us, a car full of rebellious teenagers and nervous energy. A friend in the back asked if it was a bad omen but stopped short of suggesting we turn around. Peer pressure overrides both superstition and common sense. We were committed, no turning back.

Five high-schoolers packed the old Ford, and loud electronic music suffocated meaningful conversation. We all laughed at his comment, more as an attempt to reassure ourselves than to mock his doubt. Our genius plans looked quite different in the dark of night.

Our destination was a rave in Omaha, Nebraska. World famous DJs headlined the all-night festival and we resolved not to miss out. Unfortunately, our parents did not agree. We lived four hours away and, to them, sending seventeen-year-olds on a late-night road trip to another state to attend a music scene infamous for drug use just didn't seem wise. While their rationale feels quite prudent to my adult self, my teenage perspective considered it a grievous injustice.

One of our friends received permission to go. The rest did not. This provided a fork in the road between our desires and our parent's wisdom. Rather than obey, we each told our parents we planned to stay the night at our friend's house. He told his parents we were allowed to go. It was the perfect crime. Or so we thought.

Sneaking off to another state is a bit risky for a high-schooler, and each new mile-marker increased the foreboding. Deep down, we knew it was wrong to travel this road, but once we started to drive it would require quite a bit of courage to turn the car around. We kept going.

The first sign of trouble occurred halfway into the drive, when we heard a soft thumping noise. It faintly conflicted with the beat of the music, at this point a nuisance more than anything else. We turned up the volume. Problem solved.

Fifteen minutes later, the noise grew too loud to ignore. We pulled over to look under the hood. I'm not sure what we expected to find, but everything looked good to our amateur eyes. It took a few nervous attempts to restart the engine until the motor finally roared to life. We'd hoped in vain the detour would magically fix the problem. It did not. We still kept going.

Wisdom would have turned the car around a long time ago, or never left in the first place. The loud sound reached such intensity, even the most stubborn young males could not deny the severity of the problem. We turned around, but it was far too late. The entire vehicle shook like a jackhammer. After ten minutes, we heard one last bang as the engine finally blew up, and the piercing noise was replaced by an eerie stillness.

The car coasted down the interstate and left us stranded on the side of the road, stuck somewhere between the familiarity of our home and the excitement of the rave. Maybe shooting stars are omens after all.

We still thought we'd get away with our ill-fated trip and called my friend's dad to pick us up. Our hopes were dashed when he arrived hours later. The look on his face said it all; he simply informed us he called our parents to let them know what happened. It wasn't a fun night.

I didn't know it at the time, but my act of rebellion sums up a much broader theme in my life. I'm guessing the same holds true for many of you, even if you navigated the journey with less stupidity.

I grew up in the heyday of the Christian Right, an era of strong Christian influence on society, but the world was shifting under my feet. It's taken me years to put words to it. Christian culture appeared deeply ingrained in the American culture, despite its many challengers. The Hippie Movement of my parent's generation proved powerless to shift the prevailing worldview. Evangelicalism roared back, stronger than ever. Fast-forward to today to see that things are changing, perhaps at a more fundamental level, and I grew up right in the middle of it.

Church life and Christian culture marked my formative years. Veggie Tales, conferences, Christian music, harvest parties, and summer camps all shaped my faith. Past generations experienced the trauma of a broken world firsthand. They didn't want their children to experience the same pain, so they created a new Christian subculture and designed it to be a bubble you never had to leave. A sanctified alternative existed for just about everything. I'm still grateful for much of it.

Blame the internet. Or an insular church culture that grew too intense and legalistic. I'm not sure exactly what sparked it, but my generation started looking outside the walls. In studying the broad arc of history, this was nothing new but rather the by-product of a much larger trend which has shaped the western world for centuries. We're part of a larger story.

In my teen years, my friends and I started exploring the various counter-cultures thriving at the edges of society. Punks, skateboarders, ravers, and whatever else existed in the 90s. At one level, it was completely unremarkable. These types of groups have always existed in the shadows, and curious teenagers have always found them. Many eventually found their way back into the religious fold after a few wild years, or decades, and life continued as before.

When I stepped into smoky coffee shops for a show, or warehouse parties for a rave, I saw a different world from my upbringing. Drug use and an anything-goes ethos defined the underground scene, but it was still shaped by a moral compass. The catchphrase of peace, love, unity, and respect pervaded the culture. It provided a break from mainstream America, and a safe refuge from its problems. I resonated with its simple profession of Humanist morality but had no idea what it represented.

Two roads diverged in front of me, but I found identity in both. Rather than choose a path, I tried to keep a foot on either side. I loved God, and I embraced the surrounding culture. Peace, love, unity, and respect all seemed to fit my faith. Why did I need to pick one culture over the other? Besides, I thought it was cool that people felt free to express themselves. It felt like a healthy counterbalance to the stuffy, somewhat judgmental Christian culture present in many churches throughout the country.

I still sincerely believed it was possible to stand in both worlds. I didn't want to remain trapped within Christian culture, but I also didn't want to fully abandon it.

Time provides perspective. I realize now that my internal struggle was a small symptom of a much larger shift across our nation. It wasn't just limited to the rave scene or any one subgroup. I believe in the last generation we've seen the guiding Humanist beliefs of the counterculture replace the majority Christian culture.

It has taken me fifteen years to define the internal tension. From countless conversations with people across our nation, I realize this affects a wide range of believers. This is the point of this book. *My hope is to define a historic shift in our culture, provide some language so we can understand the change, and find the Kingdom amid it all.*

Before we continue, I believe it's important to define a few terms early on since they play a prominent role throughout this book:

Cultural Christianity teaches us to behave according to God's commands, or at least look like it.

Humanism teaches us to be true to ourselves and to be good to others. It is built on the foundation that each person is fundamentally good.

The Kingdom teaches us we cannot behave rightly nor be good to others in our own strength. This is why we need the grace of God to transform us from the inside out, and to empower us to sacrificially love others.

The first chapter will discuss the ongoing worldview shift occurring all around us. The next three will highlight each of the competing worldviews, followed by a chapter which reviews historical context and then a chapter discussing views of morality.

Starting with Chapter 7, this book will shift to discuss various manifestations of this change in society: relationships and sex, self-actualization and service, the role of the church, and the primacy of the Gospel. My goal is not to exhaustively build a biblical case for each topic, but rather to show how much of our perspective results from our underlying views. The final two chapters will explore opportunities for you to respond.

The topics in this book are not new. The various arguments and counterpoints represent an ongoing dialogue spanning the last few centuries. Regardless of the historic scholarship surrounding this topic, I've found most people live largely unaware of its impact on their life. This is what motivated me to write.

The power of a worldview shift is in the way it affects the whole of society, not just the intellectual elite. As such, this is not intended to be an academic book, though I strive to present the various arguments in a fair and well-researched manner. For those wishing to explore the idea further, I've included quite a few endnotes and references to provide a starting point for additional study.

I also recognize there is a lot of nuance to this concept beyond the scope of this book. The greatest difficulty in writing was determining where to stop. Ultimately, I want it to be an accessible resource, so I've sought to maintain simplicity to keep it approachable. Normal people stand at ground zero amid the shifting worldviews, and I hope this book empowers them to greater awareness.

I'm predominately referring to modern American culture when describing the shift, but I see many of the same trends around the world. Many European countries experienced this transition a few decades earlier, and many developing countries are only beginning to feel the effects of the transition.

Our nation is on the same metaphorical trip to Omaha. We've seen the flaws with American Christianity and recognize change is needed, but I believe we're traveling the wrong road. The secular culture is equally powerless to transform the human heart. It cannot lead us into the authentic peace, love, or unity we seek.

I believe this represents an underlying tension across our society. We've changed worldviews, but it hasn't solved our anxiety or problems. In many ways, the issues seem to be getting worse, and unity appears further away than it has for generations. I agree Cultural Christianity needed to change, but I do not believe Humanism is the answer. It cannot deliver on what it promises.

Despite the obvious, we still refuse to turn off the path, no matter how much our world is shaking. Once a car is moving, it takes a lot of courage to turn it around. We are stranded somewhere between Cultural Christianity and Secular Humanism, and we don't have a clear sense of where to go next. It's the story of my life. Maybe yours as well.

Most believers remain unaware of their own journey. They find themselves questioning past perspectives they once strongly held, but they don't recognize the much larger shift in culture nor how it shapes them. I fear they also don't see just how far down the road of Humanism they've traveled.

What if there were another way? In my own struggle, I discovered I was not limited to a choice between a flawed Christian culture and the prevailing secular option. A new solution lay hidden in plain sight, found in rediscovering the teaching of Jesus.

I'm intentionally contrasting a Kingdom culture to our modern Christian culture. The Gospel message is countercultural. It confronts the flaws in Humanism and Cultural Christianity alike. It teaches a radically different view of the world by emphasizing the grace of God freely given to us, and our sacrificial love in response. All other worldviews focus on human potential and obligations.

We often fail to recognize the massive difference. I pray the coming pages will provide language and clarity regarding the views that shape many of us, and in doing so, I pray we all discover more fully what it means to live a Kingdom worldview.

Each day we spend traveling the wrong road leads us further from the power of God that leads us home. I believe most Christians genuinely desire to follow God. I also believe most Christians are primarily shaped by the perspectives of the world. This prevents us from discovering the fullness of God in our lives.

I hope to provide a balanced perspective. I've been frustrated in the past by Christians who do not fairly present their opponent's viewpoints and overlook facts that conflict with their viewpoint. I don't want to bash Humanists, nor Cultural Christians, nor anyone else. Even if I fall short, hopefully you can appreciate the attempt. We can learn from each perspective and culture while we uphold our beliefs.

Even if my analysis proves incomplete or incorrect, I hope the attempt will spur believers to reconsider what shapes their beliefs. I'm confident time will yield increased perspective, but I don't want to wait until I've already travelled too far down the road to turn around. I believe life is found in no other name but Jesus. We need to differentiate between the Gospel according to Jesus, and the gospel according to culture.

Let's behold the beauty of His Gospel, and in doing so, we'll learn more fully how to understand our culture.

CHAPTER 1

A WORLDVIEW TRANSFORMATION

Think back to your last social media argument. Maybe you resisted the urge to type, but you argued in your mind (and won!) and then relived the imaginary dispute for hours. You're probably still angry. It started innocently as you scrolled your newsfeed looking for cat photos, funny memes, and posts to reinforce what you already believe. But your brief escape was interrupted by *that* post, *that* opinion, *that* biased/ignorant/flat-wrong statement. Your blood pressure started to rise, your fingers started to type, and hopefully your self-control kicked in before you hit send. Many of us know the feeling, and we hate it. Furthermore, we agree *something is wrong*.

Why is this happening? Equally important, why does it cause such an emotional rise in me?

Part of the difficulty is our opponent. Social media is based on our social network; in other words, the offenders are people we know, people we have history with, people we trust, perhaps even love. You know they're not bad people, so how do you reconcile their horribly wrong beliefs? Sometimes it's easier to confront a stranger than understand a friend. I can project my anger onto a distant politician or media personality, but I still expect to receive affirmation in my social circle.

This dissonance forces us to confront complex questions. Are they deceived—brainwashed by a cult or fake news? Did they drastically change since you last saw them? Did they suffer a traumatic brain injury? America might seem like a divided nation, but we all stand united around the sincere conviction that our Facebook friends are crazy.

Your ideology does not inoculate you from this modern scourge. No matter what side of whatever issue you stand, you've experienced this tension. Intellectually, we affirm there are two sides to every story and believe in exposing ourselves to alternative viewpoints. Emotionally, we hate it and feel betrayed.

It's tempting to think everyone is fundamentally the same. We imagine that, after we peel back our cultural norms and then rationally embrace the latest research, it's only logical that we'll all arrive at the same conclusions. In other words, we start to think the problems in society stem from our stubborn, irrational culture and our ignorance. Solve these and we can *finally* all get along.

Maybe you claim to disagree, yet you still argue with people on Facebook. Deep inside, you think you can correct someone's wrong thinking. You subconsciously feel that if you could just expose the one glaring flaw in their argument they'd finally wake up. And thus, you start to type.

It's the internet's circle of life: a post, a reaction, a counter-reaction. Repeat with increasing emotion until an ambiguous conclusion, resolving nothing yet still adding to the collective anxiety. I don't think modern technology is the root cause of our divisiveness; instead, I think it's merely exposing what is already within us.

This underlying tension is not new to humanity, but cultural shifts are intensifying the emotions while social media is providing a grand stage for the drama to unfold, and that is unique to our era. Regardless of your online activity, you've experienced it elsewhere, such as an uncomfortable holiday conversation that steered too close to politics or the unexpectedly intense interaction at work. It's now creeping into churches, school board meetings, mom support groups, and more. Every aspect of society is gradually conscripted into some type of ideological arms race.

The root cause is not necessarily ignorance nor a decline in civility, though both may be symptoms. Instead, our problem is based in the clash between different belief systems.

COMPETING WORLDVIEWS

We all live within a *worldview*.[1] Put simply, it's the way you view the world. It's your life philosophy, your perspective, the foundation of your morals, the things so obvious to you that you've never considered whether they should be questioned. Most people live unaware of their worldview. It's just normal, how all good people think. Sure, you took a philosophy class in college, and you try to learn from other cultures, but that's just scratching the surface.

I'm a Kansas City Chiefs fan and a proud Baylor Bear. I cannot fathom how Raiders and Aggies live with themselves. I love good coffee, and I can't understand why you'd pass up the opportunity to stop at the latest craft coffee shop or ever taint your drink with sugar. These make up my perspective. I circle certain dates in the fall. I budget for coffee. I get happy with a victory and sad with a loss. Perhaps you can relate. Maybe you don't care about football; maybe you're into craft donuts instead of coffee. Your perspective might be different than mine, but you still have one.

We can laugh about our sports team, but the stakes are a lot higher when it comes to our morals, our faith, and our deepest held values. We easily recognize the surface level differences but struggle to appreciate and understand when the issue is a fundamental clash of worldviews.

I'd suggest this as the root cause of your social media conflicts. Some people are intentionally provocative, and they're the easiest to deal with. It's more difficult and emotional to handle a decent person who earnestly believes something which conflicts with your deepest beliefs. You both strive to live morally but disagree on what is moral, and generally lack the self-awareness to recognize the inherent tension.

Emotions kick in. Words are said. The thread lengthens, and someone is inevitably labeled a Communist or Nazi. Facts and reason are called upon as a witness, but feelings serve as the judge. Most of the time the dispute ends without resolution. Both sides feel they won a decisive verdict, a fact reinforced by their cultural allies, but often at the expense of a friendship. Rarely do we pause long enough to reflect on the underlying belief system that prompted the debate in the first place.

Worldviews are both culturally inherited and influenced. Unless you were raised by wolves, you received one. It's the books your parents read to you, the shows you watched on TV, the affirmation—or lack thereof—you received in school and among your friends.

We may consider ourselves freethinkers because we broke free from the bounds of our inherited culture, but have you noticed how our freethinking looks suspiciously the same as a lot of other people's freethinking? We changed, perhaps profoundly, but it was the change from one worldview to another, and it was all socially shaped.

I believe much of the shift in worldviews occurs at the societal level. We tend to change together. We don't view the world the same way we did 30 years ago, but we still view the world largely the same as the people around us today.

Social psychology professor Peter Ditto stated it this way in a *Washington Post* article, "We all think of ourselves as being these rational people. We hear evidence, and we process it. What's clear from decades of social psychological research is that people's emotions get involved in their reasoning, their motivations, their intuitions. Those shape and bias the way we process information. It's not that people believe anything they want to believe. People still think and need rationale, but the things that we feel change what we count as evidence."[2]

So, what's your worldview? Have you taken time to define it? Does it align with what you claim to believe?

THE KINGDOM WORLDVIEW

Let me be upfront: I'm a devout Christian. I pray my faith shapes my worldview. This book is written predominately for other Christians as they grapple with their worldview within a culture that doesn't necessarily align. However, I still believe a nonbeliever will benefit from an increased awareness of Christian beliefs. You may not agree, but I hope this book will help you to better understand.

An awareness of the importance of worldview is not new; in fact, I believe it is a central theme of the teachings of Jesus and a core concern of the Apostle Paul. Jesus' longest recorded message, the Sermon on the Mount, was radically countercultural and focused on contrasting the way of God to the contemporary views of His listeners. Jesus intentionally shocked and offended His audience, especially in His parables, to distinguish between their worldview and the opposite views of the Kingdom Jesus was announcing.[3] He captivated their attention in order to open their eyes to a different way of living. This process is necessarily uncomfortable.

Believers in modern times feel the same conflict of living within a competing system. Sometimes we feel guilty for our lack of social conformity, while at other times we feel angry at our lack of full belonging. Every person longs for acceptance. We want to live within a culture that reinforces our beliefs and identity. It's a natural desire, but leaves open a big question: Where do we find this?

Jesus' subversive message called His disciples to create a new culture. We find our belonging in Him and no longer in the cultures of this world. His earliest disciples lived in a world of establishment Judaism, religious fundamentalism, cosmopolitan urbanites, and nationalistic terrorists. Amidst these ideological torrents, they created something altogether different, and as a result, they too lived in tension with the world. At times it led to violent persecution, elsewhere it prompted compromise, and most commonly, resulted in a subtle irritation.

The modern Western worldview tends to downplay the communal orientation of Christianity. We analyze most of life through an individualistic lens. This oversight causes us to lose sight of a core aspect of our faith: This new culture is meant to be lived together. Believing is belonging; we leave our former tribe and step into Christ's body. Joining the new means no longer receiving full acceptance in the old.

Worldview is shaped socially, whether we realize it or not. The influence of the people around us deeply impacts how we think. We like to believe that we've developed our perspective purely from objective reasoning, but this is a fallacy. The way you think is largely determined by the way those around you think. That's why Christian community is so important. Modern individualism overlooks this profound truth.

Our social nature was not an accidental design flaw at creation, or a result of our sin. The Western worldview might minimize its influence but cannot alter its importance. At the core of our faith lies the challenge of how we live in a world in which we do not fit. We cannot do this alone; we need other believers to live the Kingdom.

Paul led Christianity's charge to establish churches across Asia Minor and Greece. His disciples hailed from both Jewish and Greek backgrounds. This diversity profoundly impacted the Church and forced believers to confront a new set of foundational worldview questions: What is Jewish? What is Greek?

What is this new Kingdom? This led to conflict with people from all sides, and occasionally with other Christian leaders who likewise sought to define the new faith.

The New Testament Epistles teach us how a diverse set of people can unite together to live the new worldview. To do this, we need to recognize that each culture has perspectives that conflict with the teachings of Jesus. We need to recognize it, let it go, and learn to embrace a new worldview. This process is difficult but necessary in order to see the Kingdom of God advanced.

The book of Romans is perhaps the most linear and detailed description of the new faith and remains a starting point for anyone seeking to understand the Gospel. Paul focused fully two-thirds of this epistle to describe a Christian's new worldview before issuing a single command on how to live accordingly. The book's first imperatives are found toward the end, in Roman 12:1-2, calling us to "offer our bodies as living sacrifices," and then issuing the challenge to "not conform to the pattern of this world, but be transformed by the renewing of your mind."

In other words, living right flows from thinking right, and achieving this requires an intentional transformation process. Furthermore, it assumes we will feel pressure to "conform to the pattern of this world," and overcoming this will require sacrifice. Though the specific "pattern" might look different within each unique culture, the core problem is universal.

This concern influenced Paul's intense letters to the Corinthian church. Paul harshly rebuked the church for living according to the prevailing Greek worldview, which led to a prolonged period of conflict. Their old culture continued to influence their motivations, their view of sex and relationships, and their conformity to idol worship.

Paul refused to back down, which caused him to face a steady opposition within the church who sought to undercut his authority. This line of attack becomes explicit in Second

Corinthians. The "false apostles" discredited Paul because he failed their standard for leadership, a very Greek standard. They argued he was a poor public speaker, lacked the right leadership persona, and literally didn't look like the part. These charges, and more, were intended to disqualify him from his role.

Two thousand years later, their opposition might seem absurd to us—this is the Apostle Paul, Saint Paul, the man who wrote half the New Testament, what arrogant jerks would dare oppose him? Time is often a reputation's best friend. To the Corinthians he was simply Paul, a human like the rest of us with both strengths and weaknesses.

As his opponents stated, "His letters are weighty and forceful, but in person he is unimpressive."[4] What if they were right? What if he was a boring preacher and unattractive? What if he didn't have a commanding presence? After all, their accusations may be valid.

Acts 20:7-12 is one of my favorite stories in the New Testament. Paul visited the town of Troas and the church called a special meeting to listen to the famous guest preacher. The clock struck midnight "as Paul talked on and on." Boredom set in. One man sitting in a third story window started to doze off and eventually fell into deep sleep, which caused him to fall out of the window and strike the ground dead.

Paul stopped his sermon, ran downstairs, raised the kid from the dead, and then had the audacity to keep preaching until daylight. Say what you will about my sermons, but I have yet to kill anyone with sheer boredom. If I ever do, I promise to take the hint and wrap it up. Paul was certainly a brilliant writer, but apparently not always a dynamic preacher.

Historic accounts seem to reinforce the claim that his physical appearance was unimpressive, with one ancient source describing him as "a man of middling size, and his hair was scanty, and his legs were a little crooked, and his knees were projecting, and he had large eyes and his eyebrows met, and his nose was somewhat long."[5]

Don't judge Paul's opponents too harshly. You might also struggle to follow a boring preacher with a comb-over and a unibrow. Paul was eventually forced to defend himself against these attacks, and I'm struck by the implications of his rebuttal. In 2 Corinthians 10, Paul pointedly flipped his opponent's entire argument by accusing them of judging according to the standards of this world. In other words, Paul accused them of evaluating his Kingdom leadership through the lens of their Greek worldview.

He yielded the point regarding his appearance, leadership style, and communication. These topics are deeply personal, and yet Paul felt no need to defend himself. Whether true or false, he deemed the charge irrelevant. His opponent's entire thought process conflicted with the Spirit because they still lived under their old worldview, and they lacked the awareness to see it.

DEMOLISH THE STRONGHOLD

In 2 Corinthians 10:3-6, Paul described the foundational problem with the following metaphor:

Though we live in the world, we do not wage war as the world does. The weapons we fight with are not the weapons of the world. On the contrary, they have divine power to demolish strongholds. We demolish arguments and every pretension that sets itself up against the knowledge of God, and we take captive every thought to make it obedient to Christ. And we will be ready to punish every act of disobedience, once your obedience is complete.

To understand this passage, you need to recognize Paul's illustration of a military siege of an enemy castle. He reveals that this represents the "arguments and every pretension ...

against the knowledge of God." In other words, the stronghold is our old way of thinking, our cultural worldview.

A victory was never complete if an enemy castle stood in the middle of disputed territory. So it is with us. If Jesus is your King, you need to give Him full reign, but this cannot happen if a stronghold remains in your mindset. There is a battle for your worldview.

In ancient warfare, once a stronghold was demolished, the invading army took their enemy captive and forcefully asserted their rule by "punish[ing] every act of disobedience." It's a vivid illustration, however intense it may sound to us. Paul challenged believers to tear down their old way of thinking, take captive the lingering thoughts, and then learn to live according to their new faith.

Paul is clear that "we live in the world." The battle is not won through withdrawing from society. Nor is the battle won with worldly weapons—manipulation, power struggles, political authority, and more. Though they professed Christ, some Corinthians still lived according to Greek standards. They neglected to deal with their stronghold, and as a result, it shaped their view of everything else.

Paul's choice of a military illustration is significant. This process is a battle; it's active and anticipates opposition. If you aren't demolishing the stronghold, the stronghold continues to rule you.

Back to my question, what's your worldview?

Have you actively waged war? Do you consistently take thoughts captive? Can you define your stronghold? If not, then I'd suggest your stronghold probably defines you. Do you evaluate life, even the Word of God, according to cultural standards? Or do you judge culture by the Word? Do you stick to mere appearances? Or go deeper to the root?

The problem with this passage is in the application. Interpreting Paul's writing is simple; interpreting our culture is difficult. We can theoretically acknowledge we have a stronghold, but to truly win the battle we need to discern what it is and how it affects our thinking. Only then can we take thoughts captive.

Every culture has a worldview. I believe each culture has beautiful attributes which uniquely display God's character. I also believe each culture is marred by strongholds which hold us back from fully knowing Him. Applying this message looked differently for first-century Greeks than it did for first-century Jews. Fast forward a few millennia to find different applications for those raised under Islam, Hinduism, secular America, and conservative Christianity. We all inherited a worldview, and with it a stronghold—the same underlying problem but a different application.

I find it far easier to see the wrong thinking in a different culture than it is to see in my own. I've traveled extensively and readily identified the problem elsewhere—the oppressive treatment of women, the idol worship, the debauchery—but my vision is clouded when I look in the mirror back home. My friends overseas probably feel the same way. They see through our pretensions easily enough, but somehow miss their own.

What's your worldview? Do you see your stronghold? Return to these questions as a reference point throughout the rest of this book. It's my hope that each chapter will help you recognize your current worldview, and perhaps serve as a catalyst to more fully embrace a Kingdom worldview.

CULTURAL CHRISTIANITY AND SECULAR HUMANISM

Modern America, and perhaps the Western World as a whole, is in the midst of a worldview transition in which Cultural Christianity is being replaced by Secular Humanism. I believe this shift, though long in the making, has only recently reached a tipping point that now dictates our nation's primary ethic and culture.[6]

If you're older than forty, you probably grew up under Cultural Christianity, and you might find this transition profoundly disorienting. If you're younger than forty, Humanism might be the only worldview you've ever known, and you may struggle to understand the thinking of an older generation.[7] This affects our relationships, ethics, viewpoints, and even our Facebook fights.

We readily experience the symptoms of this clash but consistently fail to discern the root cause. We might feel it, but we're not able to define it. For those who strive to live a Kingdom worldview, however imperfectly, we especially feel stuck amidst this titanic clash, not completely agreeing with either view.

I'm technically an old millennial who grew up in the gap between generations. I'm old enough to remember life before the internet yet young enough to be technologically fluent. I've watched the vestiges of Cultural Christianity crumble around me, much of which I cheered in an anxious sort of way. As much as I don't want to go back to what was, I don't see what's emerging as a solution, just a different set of problems. I feel stuck in no man's land, unwilling to seek refuge in the ideological trenches on either side. Perhaps you feel the same.

I'm tired of online mobs trying to force us to choose sides. I'm tired of being misrepresented in the media, the same tired charactiture some Cultural Christian is always eager to perpetuate on cable news. I'm tired of being treated like some rare ideological species for elite coastal reporters to visit on their brave forays into the evangelical heartland before settling back into the comfort of their Park Slope condominium.

As much as I don't like it, maybe this is how it's meant to be. What if the very essence of a Kingdom worldview is that you don't fit? Living as an alien and stranger is inherently uncomfortable. Pilgrims aren't supposed to settle.[8]

Much of our problem is the similarity between the competing worldviews. I think it'd be easier if the surrounding culture were radically different, because the stark contrast would reinforce what is distinctly Christian, though perhaps at a significant price. Instead the competing belief systems appear similar enough to almost believe it's all the same. Only minor compromises are needed to find a warm embrace on one side or the other.

Well-meaning people often seek to bridge this short gap by appealing to a universal moral code. Their emotional appeals speak the words of *pluralism* but the message of *universalism*. Pluralism, in a political sense, teaches that people from various faiths and worldviews can adhere to their beliefs and still live at peace with their non-believing neighbors. I completely agree.

By contrast, universalism downplays the exclusive nature of competing beliefs, preaching that we all believe the same basic things and worship the same God, just with a different name. Universalism does not seek to suppress faith, nor even discredit it—what you believe is fine, if it stays personal. But when faith influences your public life, it's suddenly seen as a barrier toward peace.[9]

Believe what you want as long as you act like a Humanist. I find it tragically ironic that what started as an attempt to bridge differences often devolves into shaming people for their wrong views.

I am not accusing anyone of a malicious attempt to snuff out faith; instead, I'm pointing the finger at well-intentioned ignorance. I believe we need to rediscover how to get along in a divided society, but this will not occur by forcing people to abandon their deeply held beliefs. I've made friends with fundamentalist Muslims and devout Hindus. We clearly disagree on serious issues, but still respect each other. Clarifying our differences doesn't hinder our relationship. In many ways it helps us get along.

I believe we can live according to a Kingdom worldview while surrounded by a society of people who do not, but we must deeply anchor our beliefs. Depending on which worldview influences you the most, it's natural to start believing your cultural worldview is the same as the Kingdom's. This step is especially dangerous because it tempts you to stop considering you ever inherited a stronghold in the first place. Though you'll feel at peace with society, this compromise will come at a steep price. You'll gain acceptance at the expense of missing the fullness of the knowledge of God.

Let's instead walk the more difficult road by embracing the charge to demolish our stronghold, to tear down old worldviews and rebuild according to the ways of Jesus. To do so, we need to learn to distinguish between Cultural Christianity, Humanism, and the Kingdom. And we need to recognize that living our faith will come at cost.

Cultural Christianity and Humanism are both fundamentally man-made and man-centered. Neither is the transformed mind of the Kingdom, and thus neither will lead to the fullness of life. The Gospel is mankind's only path to truly thrive.

CHAPTER 2

CULTURAL CHRISTIANITY

The decline of Cultural Christianity is a significant event in our nation's history, and it is deeply painful for a large number of people. The social environment is changing in profound ways and will require a long adjustment process. Regardless of how this affects you, it's important to recognize how it impacts others. This will help you to better understand our world, and hopefully extend grace to those grappling with the rapid pace of change.

The process is similar to the way we adjust to a new climate. Have you ever visited a desert? Or the tundra? Or a rain forest? I've spent time in the steamy jungles of Sri Lanka, the cold of Siberia in the winter, and harsh heat of the Persian Gulf in the summer. It boggles my mind that people survive the weather. But for the locals, it's just normal. Think of the most extreme climate shift you've experienced. Mine was a trip to South Asia.

I walked out of the plane and each step down the ramp stairs felt like a further descent into Dante's Inferno. Heat radiated off the pavement, nearly one hundred degrees before noon. Humidity completed the misery. The contrast to the cool interior of the airplane was suffocating.

Though friends warned me about the legendary heat in this rural area, I confidently assumed my Texan blood could handle it. This now felt like a serious miscalculation.

The purpose of my trip was a meeting with a remarkable group of local believers and their fast-growing network of churches. A beautiful community, but they lived in a furnace. Air conditioning was unheard of in this village. By mid-afternoon, the heat hovered over 110 degrees. Their small fan provided the only respite.

The temperature "dropped" into the low nineties that night. My only hope for sleep was under the stars. As I lay in my cot and gazed at the night sky, I felt privileged to build these new relationships a world away. But at the same time, my body seemed in danger of evaporating.

The next day I returned to the comfort of my host city. The temperature was back to a normal range, at night dropping all the way into the upper sixties, and air conditioning was plentiful. It felt like paradise.

A family from the village traveled to the city to attend a training with me, and I was surprised to see my new friends were bundled up. Coats, stocking caps, the whole works. I discretely asked another friend what was going on. He told me this was their first trip away from the village, and it suddenly hit me that this, nearly seventy degrees Fahrenheit, was the coldest weather they'd ever experienced. What was comfortable to me was extreme for them. I found the reverse to be equally true.

We each have a normal range of temperature, highs and lows to which we easily adjust. But there is a whole other spectrum that is outside our range, so hot or cold it's hard to fathom.

This is a fitting metaphor for a worldview. There is a range of normal expression, good and bad, highs and lows, we adjust to, but it's hard to imagine anything beyond. Our background temperature is what we've always known; it is so normal to us that we barely recognize it's there—unless the climate changes and forces us to confront a new normal. This will be uncomfortable.

Most Christians feel the cultural temperature changing, but we don't always have the words to describe it. There is a new range of morality and new standards in order to maintain social standing. As we adjust to the new climate, I believe that to recognize the worldview we're now entering, we first need to understand what we're leaving.

Cultural Christianity was firmly anchored as the moral foundation of the United States since its founding. This worldview acknowledges God as the supreme authority and is primarily focused on living according to His commandments. It was a good starting point, but the emphasis on the moral code eclipsed the importance of grace, leading to a heavy focus on external behavior. A wide range of theological beliefs exist under its umbrella, and though they might disagree on doctrinal statements, they still adhere to the same basic worldview. This determined the range of normal for a long time.

The basic definition of Cultural Christianity is this: Behave according to God's commands ... or at least look like it. The accountability is primarily horizontal, the way others perceive you. Within this system there is strong pressure to live morally and fulfill the appropriate spiritual and cultural obligations. Less emphasis is placed on what you actually believe or how it affects your heart.

A friend recalled visiting an amusement park with his extended family as a child. During a surface-level conversation with a park employee, they somehow discovered he intended to work on Easter Sunday. The tone of the conversation abruptly shifted. My friend's relative was appalled and sternly rebuked the young man, a perfect stranger, for neglecting "the Lord's Day."

There was no attempt to discuss his core beliefs, his relationship with Christ, or any other internal matter. The problem was his behavior, not his faith. Believe what you want, just keep it to yourself and be sure to put up the right appearances.

During my years at a Christian university, classmates regularly skipped church on Sunday morning but still had the presence of mind to wear their Sunday best to lunch at the cafeteria. If you didn't make it, at least don't make it obvious.

Your marriage may be falling apart, but you should sit next to each other at church and keep things quiet. You might live with a pornography addiction, but as long as it's kept under control, or at least hidden, it's not a big deal. Greed, gluttony, and slander will remain largely unaddressed. At times the standard is much more cultural than Christian, and the lines between the two remain blurred. God's ideals are affirmed, but in practice, some are emphasized while others are forgotten.

Cultural Christianity dominated America for centuries, though not everyone was a committed Christian. Some of the founders were Deists who believed in God and His created order but did not affirm the tenets of the faith, while others were deeply committed believers. Even though personal beliefs varied, the majority culture was grounded on living morally as defined by Scripture.

Religious freedom is the defining feature of American Christianity, and an incredible breakthrough in human rights. It came as a result of a compromise between the founders. I believe it's a powerful legacy and should serve as a guiding principle as we navigate a new set of challenges.

The Separation of Church and State was a policy advanced by Deists and radical Baptists alike. It ensured the State was not used to promote any one denomination or faith. The freedom from State involvement allowed for a rapid expansion of churches and dramatically increased religious involvement.

Despite this policy, the social climate was largely shaped by a Cultural Christian worldview. The laws of the State were shaped by the Christian moral system, the customs of the State used Christian symbols, and God remained visible throughout every level of society. No serious attempt was made to untangle the two until much later.

Things are shifting. Cultural Christianity is rapidly losing its social influence in the United States. Nearly a quarter of the nation now identifies as religiously unaffiliated, doubling in size from just ten years ago.[10] Our climate is changing at a fast pace, and for many, it's very uncomfortable.

Some have read this data to herald the death of Christianity as a whole. These claims misrepresent the real story because they fail to distinguish between active Christians and cultural Christians. The percentage of self-identified Evangelicals hasn't changed much, it's the less committed that appear to leave the faith in droves.

What is happening is a decline in Cultural Christianity. A generation ago, the vast majority of people still affirmed their Christian heritage, even if it was not a significant part of their life. This is increasingly no longer true. Ed Stetzer is a researcher who has extensively studied church history and current trends. He describes this phenomenon, saying:

> The church in the West—the United States included—is in transition right now … But transitioning is not the same as dying, particularly if you hold the belief that Christianity is represented by people who live for Christ, not check "Christian" on a survey form. Most believers likely realize that though 86 percent of Americans checked the "Christian" box on a survey in 1990, the population was not made up of that many genuine followers of Jesus. For many, the idea of being Christian and being American are one-in-the-same. But the church defines "Christian" differently than culture at large, and the distinction is an important one to make.[11]

Christianity is alive and well, but society is changing, and believers certainly feel it.

Many believers have correctly predicted this transition

and sounded the alarm accordingly. These warnings often carry a dark tone, even apocalyptic, as it mourns a nation adrift from its spiritual mooring. Whether explicit or not, the message focuses on the need to return to a better time in our nation's past, to return to Cultural Christianity.

This message is common in church circles, but increasingly falls on deaf ears—even as the prophecy is fulfilled around us. Few dispute the change is happening, but many disagree with the call to return to a "better time." The warnings of the past generation tended to interpret the decline of Cultural Christianity as a grievous threat to society, but modern believers are increasingly ambivalent.

A common retort asks about the genocide of native peoples, the slavery, and the Jim Crow laws of the last centuries. Is that the better time? Sure, the church experienced less tension with the surrounding society, sexual morals aligned with culture, and religious symbols were more commonplace, but did this represent the ideal Kingdom taught by Jesus and Paul? This rebuttal deeply resonates with a new generation of believers, cementing our unwillingness to go back. It also leaves a major question unanswered: If we don't go back, where do we go?

Christians don't want to return to the racism of that era. In fact, it was often devout Christians who led the initiatives to end these various forms of oppression in the first place. The story is more complex than the competing revisionist histories presented by both Cultural Christians and Humanists. The Evangelical narrative of a dark and drifting society is losing steam, but Christians have yet to replace it with something that more accurately describes our reality. We feel the change acutely, and as we wrestle with the implications, I worry we don't even have the words to discuss what we're experiencing.

With any transition there is loss. Society has changed rapidly in the last few generations—shifts from an agrarian to knowledge economy, rural to urban living, and a Cultural

Christian to Humanist worldview, each fundamentally altered our way of life. Like all changes, these created winners and losers.

Novelist Wendell Berry exposes the conflicting emotions of this change throughout his works, especially for those left behind. He uses the word "membership"[12] to describe the close community experienced in small town America, reminding us that while some people embraced the thrill of trading in their "narrow" existence for the opportunities in elite education and megacities, those who stayed home suffered through the steady loss of members. One way of life was destroyed so another could emerge.

This is a death by a thousand cuts, and I believe also captures the sense of loss felt by many Christians. To use Berry's illustration, believers watched their "membership" decline to such an extent that eventually the club was bought out by new owners. Humanism is now in charge and they've changed the locks, leaving Christians on the outside looking in and wondering where they fit in this new order.

There is a real, human element to this, a deep sadness in watching your home church gradually shrink in size because it's unable to keep up with the rapidly changing demographics of the neighborhood. Kids no longer roam the halls and each empty pew holds the ghost of someone who moved on long ago. The pain deepens when the doors finally close and the once vibrant community fades into memory. Eventually, the building itself is bought and reopened as a trendy new restaurant—a fitting metaphor of a house of worship turned into an altar of materialism.

This loss is further felt as cultural symbols and traditions gradually diminish with new generations and once-agreed-upon values are now widely viewed as problematic. The trend is not absolute, some places change slower than others, but the movement is nonetheless felt. Active believers may represent the same percentage as they did decades ago, but the climate they inhabit is quite different.

Grief is hard to define. It's easy to find blog posts and news stories that strive to expose the church's historic problems and the conflicting moral views of Evangelical Christians, especially in politics. While some points are valid, I believe they miss the human element. Change is difficult, and people don't always respond rationally. This does not excuse Cultural Christianity's many flaws. Its death is inevitable and is necessary for a new Kingdom worldview to emerge within the Church, but I hope we can write a fitting obituary.

It's easy for us to point out the glaring hypocrisy from our Cultural Christian past. But I wonder if we've lost more than intended in our eagerness to distance ourselves from the sins of our forefathers.

To be clear, I'm not an apologist for Cultural Christianity. In many ways I believe it represents a greater hindrance to the Gospel than Humanism, but in this postmortem, I think we need to evaluate the positive alongside of the negative.

THE POSITIVE

There is an important principle behind the success of Cultural Christianity we need to remember: Doing things God's way creates an environment for people to thrive. God created us, loves us, and wants us to experience a full life. If these claims hold true, then the key to thriving in life is by following the directions of our Creator. His commands are not burdensome because they are for our good, even if they're not easy to embrace.

I frequently issue directions to my children. Sometimes they understand the wisdom behind my instructions. Other times they chafe under what feels unfair. They need faith that I genuinely have their best in mind. I love surprising them with a trip to get ice cream or a visit to the zoo. But I also demand they eat their carrots and do their chores. I swing from a cruel tyrant to a hero within the span of a few minutes.

Some of my commands bring immediate happiness, others position them to thrive in later years. All of it is for their good. If this holds true for flawed man, how much more in our walk with God?

The extent to which we do things God's way is the extent to which mankind will flourish in this life. The rise of Humanism is proof of this, as it tries to hold to (many of) God's commands but without acknowledging God. His ways simply work. They always have and always will.

While this ideal of thriving was not always realized within Cultural Christianity, God's Word was still theoretically upheld as the standard. In addition to defining morality, it also provided a place for reform. Society regularly drifted from God's ways over the last few centuries by tolerating inexcusable forms of injustice.

In these moments, Christians consistently spearheaded the call for reform. They saw the disparity between the love, mercy, and justice of God and the oppression within their culture. Their faith prompted them to take controversial stands, often at great personal expense, to call society back to the ideal.

Slavery was mostly abolished across Christian Europe following the collapse of the Roman Empire. Transitioning a society in which half the population lived as slaves into one of near complete emancipation is one of the more under-appreciated triumphs of the Catholic church. But the rise of Colonialism in the sixteenth century reintroduced this historic injustice, and imported African slavery was gradually adopted throughout the West. The trade was lucrative, and the economic considerations outweighed the moral. Over ten million slaves were exported from Africa in a journey that killed more than one in ten people, many on British ships. The journey and destination alike were indescribably brutal, and society turned a blind eye.

In the late eighteenth century, a rising British politician named William Wilberforce was born again. He grew up in a Culturally Christian family who embraced the worldview of the time which denounced any type of devout faith as enthusiasm, especially within the upper strata of society. Wilberforce was exposed to Methodist teachings in grammar school, a development that so concerned his family they forced his transfer to avoid the harmful influence. Their decision proved successful as throughout his teens he gradually conformed to the predicable path of England's young elite.

But an exposure to faith is difficult to cure. By his mid-twenties, William Wilberforce began re-exploring the teachings of Jesus, leading to a dynamic conversion experience and ultimately altered the trajectory of his life. He knew the hostility awaiting him back in Parliament due to his newfound faith. After a period of prayer and seeking counsel, Wilberforce determined to return to his old position with a new purpose.

The slave trade provided a significant source of revenue for England and, by this time, lay deeply ingrained in the economy and culture. The primary opposition to slavery arose from devout Christians, whose radical viewpoints marginalized them from the main currents of society. Wilberforce decided to use his influence to bridge the gap.

His quest sparked a twenty-year fight to end the slave trade throughout the empire. The decades-long battle transformed public opinion and created a cascading effect throughout the world, which ultimately ended one of the great blights of the modern era. Prior to his conversion, some believed Wilberforce had the inside track toward the office of Prime Minister.[13] His "radical" views sabotaged this opportunity for power, leaving him a legacy altogether different, and far greater.

The entire social fabric of society was transformed within a generation, and it all started with a few Christians who lived according to God's Word.

This story exposes both the great strengths and weakness of Cultural Christianity. The commitment to the Word of God sparked reform in the midst of great injustice. The subsequent re-ordering of society realigned culture according to some of the core teachings of Jesus—love, serving, and equality. By living accordingly, every aspect of society thrived in ways unimaginable at the time. Even the economy, so dependent on forced labor, exceeded the wealth of the past. The degree to which we do things God's way is the extent to which we thrive.

THE NEGATIVE

But this story also demonstrates one of the great problems with Cultural Christianity: hypocrisy. Peel back the thin religious veneer and sometimes the culture looks more like a tragic parody of its ideals than the Kingdom culture of Jesus. Christian society often rejected biblical principles that conflicted with personal, economic, or political priorities. The slave trade was one of the most extreme examples of the problem, but the same flaw is evident throughout Christian culture.

We've all seen it: The smiling church on Sunday morning that turns into an angry brawl at the business meeting; the subtle racism of the people who challenge us to uphold the dignity of life; the politicians and business leaders who quote Scripture in public only to turn around and perpetuate injustice to advance their career; the pastor who rails against sin from the pulpit or television only to be caught in it himself; and the church board members who then try to cover it all up.

We've witnessed the church-going families who faithfully attended each Sunday, only to discover their home was rife with hidden abuse. We've seen people turn to the church for help in their greatest brokenness, their infidelity, and their addiction, only to find a cold shoulder. The worldview cared more about preserving a culture than it did Christianity, and that was its biggest problem.

It's easy to grow disillusioned after living through a few church splits, moral failures, or financial scandals—experiences so common that most Christians can relate. In some ways, I think it's remarkable that Cultural Christianity survived this long.

Over the last few decades, many strong believers recognized the flaws of Cultural Christianity. The fire and brimstone teaching of earlier generations is hard to find in modern pulpits. Most major evangelical groups now strongly emphasize genuine faith, grace for life's challenges, authentic relationships, racial unity, and a positive impact on society.

The decline of Cultural Christianity is as much from within as it is without. I believe many believers fear a return to this old worldview more than the rise of Humanism.

THE FATAL FLAW

All worldviews have the same problem: They rely upon the power of men and women to achieve their ideal. In Cultural Christianity, the ideal was mostly in line with God's Word, and this made the flaw hard to see.

You cannot behave your way into the Kingdom. This is the essence of the Gospel message. I need the grace of God to forgive my past and His Spirit to empower me for the future in order to live His ideals in the present. Behavior modification simply won't do the trick.

When you cannot behave in a society that emphasizes behavior, your only option is to pretend. Rather than authentically share their struggle at the risk of being ostracized, many people instead learned to put on a good face and carry on. Behave according to God's Word ... or at least look it.

This approach still casts a long shadow over the church. Many believers grew up in this climate, but its influence is waning. Fewer Christians than ever still live within this worldview; it describes our past more than our present. We may be glad to finally throw off one stronghold, but I worry we've already begun embracing a new one.

CHAPTER 3

HUMANISM

Watching a Broadway production in New York City is an experience unlike any other. My wife and I stepped out of the theatre into the pulsing lights of Times Square following two hours of pure entertainment. We spent several days in the city to celebrate our anniversary and watching *Wicked*, the legendary musical, was the highlight.

As we relived the show, my wife paused abruptly, "that was all Humanism, wasn't it? The whole message was pure Humanism." I slowly nodded. Though I had been bringing up the topic of worldview with increasing frequency over the past months, I was so caught up in the experience that I missed it.

The plot re-imagines the Land of Oz, and with it our perspective of the familiar characters. The villain of the book is the hero of the play. We learned the Wicked Witch was bullied because of her green skin and feared due to her power. An established hierarchy twisted her attempts to do good and found in her a convenient scapegoat to reshape the world according to their homogenous designs.

Our hero lived a flawed life, but not evil. She learned to embrace her power, find freedom, and help others shed their counterfeit morality to step into their authentic self. Emotional songs punctuated the show and called into question our own identity. How much of our perspective is based on blaming convenient targets?

What is good? What is wicked?

The train rumbled along deep underground as I wrestled with my wife's observation. At one level, I didn't disagree with *Wicked's* message. We should reject any attempt to marginalize or scapegoat. We should look past appearances. I considered human history, and the message seemed forceful. It described the Christians burning in Nero's gardens, the Pogroms, the Holocaust.

But something was missing. The story may be true but it's incomplete. And that's the difficulty with Humanism.

Before I explain, let me first describe the belief system. Most of us rarely discuss eighteenth-century philosophy in our daily lives. You learned about Humanism in history class and probably haven't considered it since.

This belief system is a man-centered worldview that believes the key to flourishing in this life is based on the power we have within us. Whether you realize it or not, it affects every part of our world.

My definition of Humanism is, quite simply: *Be true to yourself and be good to others.* The primary accountability in Humanism is internal. This worldview teaches you to thrive in this life by embracing your true self and that you don't need anyone else to do it.

Furthermore, Humanism believes people are inherently good. It rejects traditions which label certain behaviors bad, holding that these old beliefs create both internal and external conflicts for those who cannot measure up. Humanism considers this to be the greatest barrier to our progress. Consider the "wicked" witch's green skin. The color itself was not the problem, instead it was how others reacted to it. People feel guilty when they cannot conform, and others add to the misery by stigmatizing those who don't fit. She was forced to lash out because of others' judgments, not her own flaws.

Humanism's solution is to empathize with the uniqueness of each person and to remove the stigmas. Do this, and we'll create an environment for people to thrive. The only absolute morality is to be good to others, not our arbitrary traditions. We all must discover our unique path to a full life, and we need to show kindness to those we walk alongside.

The philosophy is everywhere in modern culture: "Chase your dream." "Follow your heart." "Embrace your passion." "Don't let anyone hold you back." "You don't need anyone or anything else." "Live your best life." "You only live once." "Do what feels right." These phrases, and countless more, proselytize the Humanist gospel.

This message forms the essence of motivational speaking. The category "self-help" succinctly captures Humanism's point. Help yourself because only you can. Take control of your life and go become the person you want to be.

Start looking for it and you'll find these phrases at every turn. Think back to the last movies you watched, the last story you read, even your kids' board books. Humanism is now the background climate of our culture.

Here's the challenge: I don't entirely disagree with the message. I believe God created each person uniquely. I believe He gives us dreams and passions. I believe we partner with Him by tapping into His power working within us.

Jesus taught us to show compassion. He spoke to sinful women, exposed religious hypocrisy, highlighted the kindness of hostile ethnic groups, and created heroes out of the outcasts. To use our Wicked illustration, I have no doubt He would embrace a woman with green skin and stand up for her in the face of a self-righteous mob. Humanism and the Kingdom share a lot of similarities.

The problem is what's missing. The story is incomplete. Did you catch that God is not part of Humanism's equation? Or did you get caught up in the inspiring messages? It's not anti-religion per se; instead, faith is demoted to an optional feature of the human experience. Some people find fulfillment in God, others in their sexuality, others in the arts, others in mindfulness, others in the ambition of their career—it's all fine *if it works for you.*

Humanism will support you if you find personal contentment in your spirituality. It's deceptively agreeable, which disguises its radical departure from the Christian faith. By placing man at the center, God is now a commodity rather than an authority. We don't need His power because we have our own. If there is no sin, then we have no need of a Savior.

Good Without God[14] is a book written by Harvard's Humanist chaplain and its title articulates the core belief of most Secular Humanists. It's essentially the Second Greatest Commandment without the First.[15] Humanism teaches us to love ourselves and to love our neighbor. Loving the Lord your God is optional.

Most people don't take the philosophy quite this far. After all, nearly eighty percent of Americans are religious. Instead, these worldviews exist together in a hybrid form. *Syncretism* is the term used to describe the merger of different religious beliefs, and rarely does any society fully adhere to the pure doctrine of any one faith. Medieval Catholicism merged with traditional Paganism while folk Islam still carries the old superstitions of long-dead foes.

Today, this same dynamic plays out as traditional faiths blend freely with Humanist beliefs. Recent studies by the Barna Group[17] show less than one third of Americans are born again. In a sign of modern syncretism, only sixty percent of these devout believers hold the Bible as the final authority in all its principles. Nearly one third of those who self-profess being born again do not even believe in the concept of absolute moral truth.

The survey uses the phrase "Notional Christians" to describe another set of believers who are less committed to the faith. This group is an additional forty percent of the nation's population, and of these, only one quarter hold to the authority of Scripture. Half disagree in the concept of absolute moral truth. Remember, these statistics just describe professing Christians.

This hybrid of Christianity and Humanism exists as the dominant perspective in our society. Most people live blissfully unaware of the conflict as they pull their beliefs from multiple sources, or try to fuse them together, like the famous Bible verse, "God helps those who help themselves." For the record, this is not a real Bible verse.

Though large numbers of people still profess Christianity, the Humanist worldview shapes our society. My prediction is that with each successive generation, theological beliefs will gradually align with the dominant belief system.

The data supports what I regularly experience in ministry. I connect with a wide variety of churches across America, and I'm not at all surprised by the Barna surveys. Instead, I can't figure out why it took me so long to notice something so obvious. I treated countless symptoms when it came to actual behavior and moral beliefs but failed to discern the underlying cause. Sexual ethics, politics, and the rejection of certain tenets conspire to steal the spotlight, all while the source laying deeply embedded in our worldview remains unnoticed.

We can wrestle through the symptoms all we want, but if we don't discern the root cause, it will not lead to lasting change. Many people are living the natural implications of the Humanist worldview, and we're trying to reach them through the language of Cultural Christianity. It's not working.

Our disentangling from Cultural Christianity is partially to blame. We're eager to shed the hypocrisy of the past, and rightfully so, but this limits our awareness of the present. However, I believe there is a more significant reason why something so blatant is easily overlooked.

We miss Humanism because we don't see it as an actual worldview. Since there are no formal creeds nor religious dogma, we consider it as the mere absence of belief. Or, to put it another way, we're tempted to view it as the natural perspective of those who are less religious, as though they all magically default into the same mindset.

Humanism is not religious, but it is certainly an active belief system.[18] It requires faith, holds core tenets, calls adherents to strict morality, and actively evangelizes nonbelievers. Heretical beliefs will cause an excommunication that will cost you social standing. Inquisitors eagerly prowl the internet to expose the blasphemer and mobs wait at the ready to enforce the sentence. There may be no priest, but there are saints. You can even find congregations. Its message is discipled into children and taught in schools. Zealous leaders employ their influence to advance the message in business, politics, and media.

The faith is in the power and goodness of humans. The tenets include the belief in each person's uniqueness, the call to maximize self, and the challenge to show kindness to others. The morality focuses on empathy and altruism, while also recognizing the collective effort to remove traditions that still hinder man's progress due to their antiquated views of righteousness.

Aside from directly hurting someone else, Humanism's greatest heresy is to be judgmental, even in your thoughts. If everyone is on a unique path to fulfillment, then any attempt to exalt one approach or belittle another is a direct violation of the core belief. If everyone is inherently good, then people's problems come from their environment. Judgment is considered so grievous because, to a Humanist, it is a primary reason people struggle. The assumption is that if everyone was accepting, kind, and all systemic barriers were removed, then people would be free to express their true self and, therefore, thrive.

Philosophers, poets, and playwrights form a new sainthood, a cloud of witnesses to inspire the faithful. Business leaders and politicians now routinely signal their virtue in Humanist terms. Bible verses and token church appearances have given way to taking a corporate stance on a progressive social issue for those seeking to gain credibility among the faithful.

Humanism is an active belief system and is rapidly advancing throughout our culture. Mass conversions are occurring under the religious label of "not affiliated." Sociologists and philosophers will study this in years to come and, as with all things, there is nuance and complexity involved, but the overall picture is striking.

I'm focusing on society as a whole; on an individual level, things are far more complicated. Some non-religious people reject Humanism. Some Christians freely embrace it. Muslims, Buddhist, and others advocate alternative worldviews. I'm not saying Humanism is the main influence on each person's beliefs; instead, I'm contending it's the primary influence on our culture.

Christians must adjust to this new normal. We must recognize what is happening around us and consider how much we've allowed Humanism to shape our own worldview. Which belief system shapes your actions and your perspective most? What grid do you use to make major life decisions?

In particular, we need to live aware of the pull to compromise. Humanism is not hostile to our private faith, but it will try to convert us. Its message is alluring, we don't even need to give up our religious identity. But we must cede the freedom to let our beliefs shape our actions if we want to fit into the new order. Universalism rules the day.

The language of pluralism neatly fits Humanist beliefs, but the two live in the tension between religious rights and individual rights. Pluralism supports the rights of religious communities to live in harmony despite their differences. This was the founding premise of the United States—bumpy at times, but a defining feature of our religious landscape. Protestants, Catholics, and Jews all lived side-by-side peacefully. New denominations displaced the old, all without government involvement.

I worry Humanism will not be so accommodating. Religious beliefs impose a moral code on their followers that is based on an absolute Spiritual Authority, and these conflict at time with Humanism's morals. Humanism seeks to free people from all traditional constraints, and it already functions likes a de facto State religion. Over time, I believe we'll face more hurdles to living the fullness of biblical faith.[19]

Despite my concerns, I believe we can easily co-exist. Humanism and the Kingdom share much of the same morals, along with many other faiths and worldviews. This starting point provides a lot of common ground, or as the American philosopher John Rawls described it, an "overlapping consensus."

But for this to happen, we must openly state our differences and resist the urge to cover them up. In my experience working with people from other faiths, I've found clearly articulating our distinctions empowers us to respect each other. Rather than seeking to gloss them over, we need to talk about them. This understanding allows us to passionately argue our viewpoint without attempting to suppress someone else's.

Humanism shares a lot in common with Christianity, especially within the moral code. The emphasis on concern for our neighbor and justice in society are very similar to the Christian worldview, which is built on love and charity. Individualism originated in the Christian belief that each person is created in the image of God and as a result has an intrinsic worth and beauty.[20] Reason sprang from Christian scholars in the Middle Ages, believing that if God ordered the world at creation then His order can be discovered.[21]

Furthermore, Humanism corrects many of the flaws found in Cultural Christianity. Authenticity is prized over conformity. People are valued for who they are more than how they fit. Injustice is exposed rather than covered up. Concern for the marginalized is greater than a concern for the status quo.

It grieves me that it took such a significant social shift to wake up the Church to the sin we tolerated in our era of cultural dominance. Even though large numbers of believers lived wholehearted and authentically in those years, it was never enough to shift the worldview. Humanism stole our playbook, and now we're playing catch up.

Christians should have shed light on the epidemic of sexual abuse, yet all too often, concerns were swept under the rug for the sake of an institution's reputation. Though many Christians stood on the front lines of the Civil Rights movement, many others landed on the wrong side.

The lack of authenticity was perhaps the greatest flaw of Cultural Christianity. People saw through the duplicity. The lack of heart transformation prevented meaningful behavior change. What power does the Gospel have if those who profess it look like everyone else?

Our significant places of agreement make it difficult to distinguish between the two worldviews—so much that we fail to notice the vastly different foundations. Despite our commonalities, rifts are appearing with greater frequency, and none more so than the area of sexuality.

In the summer of 2015, the Obergefell v. Hodges Supreme Court decision legalized homosexual marriage across all fifty states. More than the issue at hand, I believe it proved a decisive verdict for the direction of the nation in its long march toward Humanism.

The topic of homosexuality is deeply emotional and complex, and most of it is outside the scope of this book. However, I'm using it as an example because I believe it clearly illustrates the difference between the competing worldviews.

I hold to the traditional, biblical teaching on sexuality, and I also believe Christians need to recognize and confront our own sin in the way we treated homosexuals. In the years leading up to the Court's ruling, a spotlight was shone on the past. For Cultural Christians, homosexuality was, in some ways, considered the ultimate sin due to its overt rejection of social norms. As a result, it carried a major stigma which resulted in all types of bullying and abuse. Rather than providing a safe harbor to work through the struggle, the church often proved the worst offender.

Humanism on the other hand empathized with the pain and started viewing homosexuals as people rather than outcasts. This is the place where believers and Humanists agree. After all, Jesus modeled love and compassion for sinners while still upholding God's righteousness. Cultural Christianity failed to do this, instead choosing to hold to the moral code without regard for love or grace. It upheld a standard of righteousness, but in a sort of spiritual Darwinism, sought to banish those unable to conform rather than help them find Jesus.

If Cultural Christianity sought to ostracize, Humanism went the opposite direction and sought to normalize. The phrase "born this way" emerged as a rally cry that captured their philosophy. It's a compelling argument, after all, if someone is born with a particular orientation then why should they be stigmatized as though they did something wrong?

If you adhere to Humanism, then a person's sexuality is neutral. As long as they don't hurt anyone, then there is no problem in pursuing whatever leads to fulfillment. Therefore, if someone was "born this way" then any attempt to hinder them from living accordingly is immoral. Any internal tension they feel is not a problem with their sexuality but rather a guilt imposed by outdated religious teachings. Be true to yourself and be good to others, there is no other moral code.

This is a stark contrast to a Kingdom worldview, which teaches that there is an absolute morality which is expressed in the Person of Jesus and revealed through His Word. God created us, and He alone knows how humanity can best thrive. His standards provide boundaries to protect us, enable us to live a rich life, and reveal God to humanity. We believe God calls us to live according to His ways, in our treatment of others, and in our personal lives—including our sexuality.

However, the Bible also reveals no one can live up to God's standards in their own strength. The Doctrine of Original Sin teaches that mankind is born inherently sinful. This is the source of the internal conflict we feel, be it sexuality or any number of other issues. The problem is not the external guilt imposed by others but rather the internal conviction for our own sin. And it's the primary difference with Humanism.

The Gospel agrees people are "born this way," but disagrees with our culture on the implications. Every person on the planet is born into sin, but "this" looks different for each person. For some, "this" is a bent towards anger. For others, "this" represents greed or gluttony or sexual sin, or all the above.

The Kingdom's contrast to Humanism is how we respond to being "born this way." Humanism seeks to fix the problem by redefining right and wrong, driven by the idea that there is no consequence beyond social acceptance. This is the approach to homosexuality, as well as countless other social issues.

The Gospel is entirely different, and begins in recognizing God as the ultimate authority, not the social constructs of humanity. It recognizes both the truth of God's Word and our failure to live accordingly. No one can live a perfect life, which is why we need a Savior. Jesus alone lived righteously, and He alone paid the price for our sin. He empowers us to live *His way* despite the reality that we were born *that way*.

When we truly embrace the truth of the Gospel, we become compassionate, recognizing everyone struggles with the pain of sin—it just looks different for each person. My sin is not better than someone else's, even if it's more socially acceptable. Both lead to destruction. We should empathize with the suffering of others as they grapple with the sin inherited at birth. And we should live humbly when we recognize we're equally sinful in our natural state.

I agree with the call to live authentically, but this alone will never lead to abundant life. If you're self-centered, being true to yourself isn't helping anyone. A more authentic selfishness isn't really an improvement. Think about it. Authentic is better than fake, but it alone cannot transform. This is the fatal flaw of Humanism. What do you do if you're not inherently good? It'll make you feel better about yourself, but it won't change you.

The Humanist catchphrases sound inspirational, but they're impotent. Ultimately, if you live true to yourself then you will not be good to others. Your sin will sabotage your dreams. The Humanist message is incomplete.

Most believers grew up within Cultural Christianity and lived through its problems. We saw the need to expose the hypocrisy and rediscover the power of authentic faith. This sparked waves of revival throughout the Church and a fresh concern for our impact on the needs of our communities.

But our internal awakening paralleled the rise of Humanism in the broader culture. Both believers and Humanists alike have grown increasingly aware of the plight of the marginalized. Together, we've learned to show empathy toward people we don't understand. We've all linked arms to fight against injustice. I'm thankful for all of it, but I'm also worried we've taken it further and started to buy into the fundamental message. We can partner with our culture on a lot of issues, but we must not lose the very foundation of our hope.

I still enjoyed watching Wicked. I agreed with the message, and I'd gladly watch it again. But I'm also aware of what's missing. The solution for believers is not to weed out every catchphrase or Humanist influence in our lives. Instead, we need to live with an even greater awareness of the Gospel. When this is our foundation, everything else will rightly align; and, ultimately, we'll find the power to actually live out the ideals we all uphold.

God created us to love, to do good, to bring life, but as Scripture reminds us repeatedly, we cannot do so in our own strength. The ancient words of the prophet Jeremiah still ring true. "Cursed is the man who trusts in man and makes flesh his strength, whose heart turns away from the LORD. He is like a shrub in the desert, and shall not see any good come ... Blessed is the man who trusts in the LORD, whose trust is the LORD. He is like a tree planted by the water."[22]

Recognizing the reality of our condition is essential to truly understanding our salvation. When we understand our inability to do good, it forces us to discover the One who came to rescue us. This is the power of grace. To embrace the Humanist view of man's inherent goodness is to reject the Gospel. Attempting to redefine right and wrong is a cheap solution to the plague of sin. We might feel better about our problems, but we don't solve them. Only Jesus does that.

CHAPTER 4

THE KINGDOM

The dawn of the twentieth century carried a naïve faith in Humanism, especially for the intellectual elite. While the multitudes still held their quaint beliefs, the upper strata of academia saw change on the horizon. Inherently good, rational humans were set to lead the world into ever increasing levels of peace and prosperity. The unparalleled progress of the era validated this worldview and gave it the air of inevitability. The ignorant masses may still find comfort in their religion, but soon these beliefs would no longer be necessary. The era of religious conflicts was over. Reason and the goodness of man would now rule the day and lead mankind into an unprecedented peace.

This dream died on the bloody fields of the Somme. Reason and science, the poster children for the new worldview, did lead to economic growth. They also led to greater efficiency in killing. Mankind grew wealthy by conquering nature, but never learned to conquer themselves. The quest for power still ruled the heart. The agonizing cries in the trenches exposed the idealism for the fantasy it always was. Humanism brought prosperity but could not bring peace.

After the smoke settled, the elite determined to salvage their worldview. Too much was invested in their faith in mankind to abandon the cause after one setback. They pronounced the violence to be "the war to end all wars." They declared it an aberration in the path toward human achievement. The fallen did not die in vain, for soon a new world order would form out of the ashes to ensure it never happened again. Reason would prevail. Goodness would conquer.

Two decades later, Hitler's blitzkrieg raced across Poland. Japan brutally invaded China. The Soviet Empire continued to purge all dissent. All told, up to one-hundred million people were killed in just thirty years. The second war ended without the hope of the first. Nuclear weapons proliferated and caused a legitimate threat to the future of humanity. Though technology continued to develop at breakneck speed and scientific knowledge grew rapidly, it had no effect on human nature. No amount of learning nor any amount of science provided a cure to the problem within.

As the sun set on the twentieth century and we stepped into a new era, it amazes me that society still holds to the fallacy of believing people are born inherently good. What further proof do we need to see that we are our own worst enemy? Though many philosophers and psychologists have moved on to new theories, most of our culture continued on to fully embrace Humanism, and we still haven't resolved its fundamental problem. If anything, it's been amplified.

Sin is the natural condition of man. We see it in dictators, slavery, racism, sexual abuse, and violence. But, if we're honest, we also see it in our own hearts. It's the anger we cannot control. It's the selfishness in our closest relationships. It's the dishonesty at work. It's the inability to control our appetites. It's the root cause of our regret, haunting our quiet moments. It's the enemy within, warring against the person we strive to be. Most people can keep their sin under control, at least enough to only hurt the people they're closest to. But it's there, all the same.

This is the root problem all worldviews must address. It is the gap between our ideals and our reality. How do we overcome sin? We've looked at two worldviews so far. Cultural Christianity tells us to cover sin up. Humanism teaches that sin doesn't exist. Neither have the power to take it away. You probably know the feeling.

THOMAS' STORY

Thomas woke to a pounding headache and nausea, with only a vague memory of the prior evening. His condition worsened with each passing hour, and he grew worried. He started to vomit uncontrollably and began to panic. Something was very wrong.

He searched his medical symptoms online and quickly found the answer. A banner across the screen highlighted opioid withdrawal symptoms, and he was experiencing every single one. He looked down at the injection marks on his skin, and it all started to make sense. He ran to awaken his friend, desperate for chemical relief. A short while later, OxyContin shot into his blood stream, relief flooded his body, and the symptoms instantly disappeared. As he calmed down into the stillness of the high, Thomas stepped onto his porch to smoke a cigarette and finally confronted the truth that he was an addict.

He grew up in a typical middle-class home and, with it, the ordinary irritations of childhood. Things took a dark turn when he moved during middle school. His first year in the affluent neighborhood was lonely. He did not fit in with his classmates, and he knew it. If by chance he forgot, they quickly reminded him.

He felt their judgment due to his inability to conform. In this new world, acceptance required a certain appearance, which felt unattainable even if he wanted it. Thomas rejected this monochromatic existence and sought belonging elsewhere. He discovered a group of social outcasts who accepted him for who he was, and they preached a completely different message—just do what feels right and don't judge anyone else. The words liberated him. For a while.

His new social circle started experimenting with drugs, and for Thomas this felt right. He started smoking weed, and then moved further down the well-worn path into harder narcotics. The highs brought with them a sense of peace and stilled his buried desire for love and acceptance. He felt in control and free from the mindless conformity of the world around him.

A drug habit is expensive, so he started selling part of his stash to his friends to generate income. His clientele gradually broadened, and soon he earned hundreds of dollars per day dealing enough drugs to live comfortably while still paying for his own usage. Over several years Thomas tried, and then sold, almost every illicit drug without ever developing an addiction. This equilibrium held for a while. He barely graduated high school, and then promptly flunked out of college. But he didn't care. He didn't want that life anyway.

As he stood puffing his cigarette outside his apartment complex, the reality of his situation invaded his cloudy mind. He accepted the truth of his problem but wasn't ready to confront it. He still believed he was in control. Though more than a dozen of his friends died of a drug overdose, he believed he was smarter and stronger. He still believed doing what felt right led to fulfillment.

A short while later, Thomas was arrested for a parole violation. His time in jail forced him to completely withdrawal for the first time. It was the most miserable week of his life. His skin was on fire; his body shivered and ached. Migraines pierced his head, and he was incapable of eating. Stepping out for roll call felt like torture. Once he sobered up, he vowed to never go back.

This resolved lasted about a month. He still craved the release he found while high, and this pull was as strong as the chemical dependency. One hit turned into more, and his addiction returned, stronger than ever. This initiated a years-long cycle of cleaning up only to fall right back. He visited six different rehab centers during this period, always with the same result.

Thomas confronted the truth about his addiction, but not the reality of his flawed nature. He first moved out of his drug-dealing apartment, rationalizing his environment was the source of his problem. But every time he moved, his addiction followed. With each successive slide further into brokenness, he started to discover the real problem lay within.

His sense of control was an illusion, and the once-liberating advice of his friends was a prison. Doing what felt right was killing him. He bounced around from place to place until he finally landed in a cheap hotel. His addiction grew unsustainable. He looked out the window at the lifelong addicts living on the streets and realized it was a view into his future. He looked in the mirror and saw a man he never wanted to be. Drugs provided a temporary peace, but at a great expense. This made him desperate; it was the last exit on the highway toward his destruction. He determined to get free no matter the cost.

Though he occasionally attended church with his family, Thomas never paid attention until this last stint in rehab. He knew he needed a Savior to set him free. The rehab center was an eclectic mix of people. He saw Fentanyl addicts in their sixties, still trapped in the cycle. He saw his former customers wander through the doors. The depressing sight deepened his resolve to change. Thomas started to seek out spiritual people, read his Bible, and looked to God to rescue Him.

After sobering up for a month, he took the radical step of enrolling in a year-long, church-based recovery home. This step was unthinkable just a year earlier, but he was finally willing to do anything to find freedom. Desperation leads us to seek help in unlikely places. When we're trapped in sin, we eventually discover the cost of maintaining the status quo is greater than the price of our liberty.

One night after a worship service, Thomas radically encountered the love of God for the first time. Words cannot describe this type of spiritual experience. The love of Christ changed from a concept to a lived reality. He met Jesus. He *experienced* grace. Looking back, he realized he'd been searching for love and acceptance his whole life. Drugs merely numbed his pain and masked the emptiness in his soul. It was a cheap solution, but it was all he had.

This experience with the real, living Jesus changed everything. Thomas realized his old life could not be rehabilitated by his own strength. He could never manage his sin. His only hope was to trade in his old self for a new life in Jesus. It's the power of the Gospel. Grace and love finally set Thomas free.

Perhaps our sin is not as overt, but it's there all the same. We, too, live under the same illusion of control, believing we can find fulfillment in the things of this world. And if we travel that path, we will wake up to the same destruction.

The Kingdom worldview is entirely based on this Gospel message. Earlier, I referenced Paul's letter to the Romans. This book of the Bible clearly describes the new Kingdom worldview. I recommend it as a starting point for study for anyone seeking to build stronger foundations in their faith. The book's core message is as radical today as it was two thousand years ago. Its purpose is to remind the Church of our new identity, and thus our new way of living.

Paul's introductory statement is found in Romans 1:16: "I am not ashamed of the gospel, because it is the power of God that brings salvation to everyone who believes." The early church faced competing worldviews that claimed to lead mankind to fulfillment. But, just like today, these beliefs did not have power to set people free from sin. The man-made solutions of Paul's day were equally as ineffective as our own. We're not ashamed of the Gospel, because it alone saves. The first three chapters of Romans lay the foundation for the entire Kingdom worldview. They provide a stark contrast to every other belief system, and I believe this message alone has power to save.

As we go through them, I recognize this is a review for most Christians. If you're like me, you may be tempted to skip over it. This is our problem. Because we intellectually understand the message, we mistakenly assume we're living it. Reciting a creed is not enough to shape a worldview. We need to meditate and live this message to such an extent that it shapes our view of everything else.

ROMANS 1

The first chapter of this book frames the problem by describing the sinfulness of humans. Verse 25 reveals the root issue, that we "exchanged the truth about God for a lie, and worshiped and served created things rather than the Creator." Each worldview of man worships the created rather than the Creator. We want to be in the driver seat in our path to fulfillment. Paganism, Humanism, Consumerism, Fundamentalism, and all the other "isms" reflect this tendency.

The problem is that it doesn't work. Occasionally, our façade of control cracks to reveal the truth—the mustard gas haze covering the fields of France, the ghost trains of Punjab, and the streets of Kigali all bear witness to man's quest to serve created things. More banal consequences litter everyday life, evidenced by our rising anxiety and depression rates,[23] opioid addiction, and the pervasive sense of loneliness.[24]

Living authentically in your sin cannot bring life. Thomas discovered the hard way that doing what feels right will lead you into what is wrong. Sexual fulfillment does not last. Possessions cannot satisfy. Power will not bring happiness. Too many people spend their life chasing these things, believing it will fill their emptiness. Most live and die without ever succeeding, always finding contentment just beyond their reach. The privileged few who actually find the money, sex, and fame have it worse. They reach their destination only to discover it was a mirage, an illusion of life in the desert of their soul. This was true of millennia past and still rings true today.

The chapter ends with a blunt assessment of our condition: *Just as they did not think it worthwhile to retain the knowledge of God, so God gave them over to a depraved mind, so that they do what ought not to be done. They have become filled with every kind of wickedness, evil, greed and depravity. They are full of envy, murder, strife, deceit and malice. They are gossips, slanderers, God-haters, insolent, arrogant and boastful; they invent ways of doing evil; they disobey their parents; they have no understanding, no fidelity, no love, no mercy." Romans 1:29-30*

We worshiped the created, the things we control, but they failed to fulfill us. In our modern context, the first chapter is a powerful rebuke to the emptiness of Humanism. What is the fruit of pursuing our desires if they cannot fulfill? Does removing traditional constraints reveal our "inner goodness" or does it merely expose our emptiness? History books provide the answer.

ROMANS 2

Cultural Christians can appreciate the first chapter of Paul's letter. It reinforces the truth that sin will not satisfy. It fits their message so much so that they fail to see Paul is blindly leading them into a trap. A religious worldview stops reading after Romans 1 and jumps straight to the lifestyle commands at the end of this book. Though no one says it aloud, the basic idea is that if you keep God's commands better than your pagan surroundings, you're doing fine.

Paul spoke an entirely different message. God doesn't grade on a curve. Rather than commend the religious for their external display of righteousness, Paul instead laid an ambush.

You, therefore, have no excuse, you who pass judgment on someone else, for at whatever point you judge another, you are condemning yourself, because you who pass judgment do the same things. Now we know that God's judgment against those who do such things is based on truth. So when you, a mere human being, pass judgment on them and yet do the same things, do you think you will escape God's judgment? Romans 2:1-3

If Romans 1 is a rebuke to Humanism, then Romans 2 is a rebuke to Cultural Christianity. God is not fooled by our religious activity. He knows what lies beneath. We may go to church weekly, we may get outraged at the sin in our nation, we may speak fluent Christianese, but these will not save us.

We need to catch the forcefulness of Paul's words. Using modern terminology, it's something like this: "You claim to know the commands of God and use your knowledge to cast judgment on your neighbors. Do you realize you're digging your own grave? The very things you condemn others for doing, you're doing yourself! You might fool people, but you will not fool God. Keeping appearances is not a winning strategy in Heaven's courtroom. Not only are you guilty, but you're brazen enough to judge other people for doing the same thing."

Though Paul spoke to first century religious Jews, his concerns closely mirror our Cultural Christianity. Some people seek fulfillment in embracing their sin while others try to cover it up. Neither works.

God isn't impressed by our religiosity. Ultimately, we cannot solve our sin problem through any amount of church attendance or behavioral change. It's like a Band-Aid on a gunshot wound or a cough drop for tuberculosis; we might be able to slightly cover up our condition, but we cannot take it away.

ROMANS 3

Sin is a fatal condition. Awareness cannot cure, nor will denial resolve our flawed nature. History provides countless man-made worldviews promising to remedy the underlying disease of sin, but each proves a panacea incapable of healing us. Our efforts yield the spiritual equivalent of snake oil—we may feel better, but it's all fake. We're simply masking our fate until the fatal symptoms finally burst through.

An accurate diagnosis is the first step toward treatment. The first two chapters of Romans revealed the problem. The third provides the solution. There is nothing we can do to heal ourselves; we need a Savior.

> *For all have sinned and fall short of the glory of God, and all are justified freely by his grace through the redemption that came by Christ Jesus. God presented Christ as a sacrifice of atonement, through the shedding of his blood—to be received by faith. Romans 3:23-25a*

Jesus died so we might live. He paid the penalty for our sin and now invites us into a new life. Grace speaks of forgiveness for our past—the trail of broken relationships and missed opportunities, the regret, the hurt, the pain. Grace is also power for our future—a life no longer bound to sin, free to sacrificially love God and people.

Like Thomas discovered, our only hope is in dying to our old self and embracing the new life that comes with Jesus. We cannot reform our sin nature, so God came to kill it.

HEART TRANSPLANT

In the mid-1980s, Dwight Kroening started to feel sick. He first assumed it was the flu, but the symptoms worsened with each passing week, so he begrudgingly visited the doctor. Kroening was in his late twenties and in good health. At this age, most doctor's appointments lead to an antibiotic prescription and a note to take the day off.

This visit was different. The doctor took an X-ray and immediately grew concerned. Kroening's heart was enlarged; further testing confirmed the extent of the problem. He was diagnosed with a heart defect —his symptoms were the beginning stages of heart failure. This condition was terminal. For the young man, a routine doctor's visit pronounced a death sentence.

In a later interview with Canada's National Post, Kroening described the experience, saying "I thought, 'This is just a dream, it can't be true,' or else just give me something to do to fix it. I was told there's nothing anybody can do. They stabilized me and said, 'Go home and prepare to die.'"[25]

Kroening's prognosis gave him only a few months to live. The heart failure continued to accelerate as his life ticked down to the end. He was hospitalized and appeared to be in his last days, when Kroening was abruptly matched with a potential donor. Heart transplants were still rare at the time, but new advances in medicine improved the survival rate and extended the survivor's life expectancy to five years. The surgery was a major risk, but it was also his only hope.

He was rushed into surgery. The surgeons removed his defective heart and replaced it with a healthy one. The operation was successful. Breakthroughs in immune suppressants allowed his body to receive the new heart and, in the coming months, Kroening began his slow recovery. He traded in a dead heart for the living, and now his body had a chance.

This is a perfect analogy for sin. We're all born with a birth defect. We're all "born that way," and our disease is terminal. There is nothing anyone can do to cure our heart. Some people recognize their true condition more quickly than others. Thomas' addiction exposed his problem at a young age, while many others will go to the grave never understanding their sickness. We see the symptoms but often fail to diagnose the true problem.

The only solution to a defective heart is to receive a new one, and the only way to receive a new one is for a healthy person to die, which is why Jesus went to the cross. This was Kroening's story, and this is our story. It is central to the Gospel message. Sin, our heart disease, is incurable and terminal. No man-made effort can heal us.

Consider the other worldviews: Humanism teaches us there is no defect, though deep inside we all know the truth. Cultural Christianity prescribes treatment to manage a few of the symptoms but does not touch the real problem. Our attempts prove futile as the disease progresses to its inevitable conclusion. Our only hope is a heart donor. We need to remove our sinful, diseased heart and replace it with a healthy one.

The problem is every person on the planet is born with this same condition. We cannot rescue each other. Donor organs only work if they're healthy. This changed for us on a quiet night in the small town of Bethlehem. God Himself stepped into our world in the person of Jesus. He is the only person to live untainted by sin. He never needed to modify His behavior, because His behavior was already right. He could live true to Himself, because He truly was good.

But to be a donor, He first had to die. Jesus was executed by a collusion between the religious Jews and the pagan Romans. He chose to die so that we might live. Three days later He rose from the dead, appeared to hundreds of His followers over the following weeks, and then rose to Heaven. He alone offers a new heart, and He alone is able to save us.

This is the redemption; this is the sacrifice of atonement—death so another can live. His blood was shed so we might be healed. This gift is received by faith. A transplant recipient cannot earn his new heart; it must be accepted as a gift. Free grace for one came at a great price for another. When we commit to follow Jesus, our old self, our diseased heart, is removed and replaced with the life of God.

This is the hope Thomas found. Years of addiction could not be cured through behavior modification or even breaking the chemical bonds in his body. He needed a heart transplant, a new life only found in Jesus.

The Kingdom worldview is based on this foundation. Everything else—how we live and how we treat others—stems from this gift of grace. If we miss this, we miss the Kingdom.

A NEW LIFE

When salvation is central to our worldview, every other aspect of the Christian faith falls into place. The book of Romans goes on to reinforce that once we've had a heart transplant, we need to start living according to our new identity. Why would we ever return to our defect after we've been healed? This foundation is crucial to actually live the Kingdom worldview. We now have power to live according to God's commands—not to earn grace, but because we already have it. He alone provides the transplant. We're free to live a new life.

We cannot simply modify our behavior according to some of God's commands and expect it to save us. The problem is deep within us and, until that is resolved, no amount of human effort will set us free. The Gospel anchors the worldview of those who've received a new heart. Reducing the Christian faith to a set of morals misses the point entirely, and ultimately lacks power. Healthy living isn't very helpful if you're experiencing heart failure. Left unchecked, sin will destroy us. That's why we need a Savior.

Consider Dwight Kroening. His transplant surgery was the beginning of his new life. He was alive but was given the choice on how to live. He was not content to merely delay death a few more years; instead, he decided to work out his new heart, quite literally.

He first started to exercise. His doctors reluctantly allowed it, but they were worried; this wasn't common at the time. Kroening worked out his new heart and started competing in races, eventually moving on to full marathons. In 2009, he crossed the finish line after completing an Ironman Triathlon. A dying man rose to life and then went on to complete one of the most grueling competitions on the planet. His old heart nearly killed him. His new heart empowered him to do the impossible. He's gone on to live a healthy life, far longer than anyone could have imagined. The heart was a free gift of grace; he received it and allowed it to shape his worldview.

Consider Thomas. He found freedom from his addiction, but more importantly found freedom from his sin. He experienced new life in Jesus and found power to stay clean. He now spends his time volunteering to help other men escape drugs.

Which worldview do you live within? I'm not minimizing the importance of morals or creeds; they're significant. But right affirmation of biblical ethics or theology will not have power if it's based on man's effort. Both Humanism and Cultural Christianity miss the preeminence of the Cross and Resurrection. Let's put this at the center, and I believe everything else will fall into place.

CHAPTER 5

UNDERSTANDING THE NARRATIVES

"Wait until you see this!" my realtor exclaimed as she lifted the door to a bomb shelter. It wasn't a feature I particularly wanted, but the price was right for the rest of the house. Now I was the proud owner. Steels doors guarded the entry to my new refuge, which lay buried below ground and protected by a foot of reinforced cement.

Six months later, I finally ventured down to clean it out. Four inches of murky water lapped against my boots as vague shapes floated past, mercifully obscured by the dim lights. The previous owners took this space seriously. They hung sheetrock, wired electricity, and kept a supply of board games at the ready to stave off the boredom of riding out a nuclear holocaust.

Subterranean bomb shelters don't age well. The house had sat empty for over a decade. Years of neglect allowed rain to seep in, which then caused the walls to rot and crumble. The result was a stew of soggy plaster and dead cockroaches.

My long hours underground caused me to question the logic. Why would someone ever build a bomb shelter in Waco, Texas? This thing cost serious money. Was the salesperson just that good? I can't imagine my sleepy neighborhood was ever high up on the Soviet war-planner's target list. If they run out of targets and decide to start nuking Waco, then we're already well on our way to nuclear winter. Besides, I'd rather go out in a blaze of glory than survive the initial blast in my shelter, only to slowly die in a radioactive wasteland. But to each his own.

It seemed like common sense that this monstrosity was unnecessary, but I have the luxury of hindsight. The first owners lived in a different perspective. John F. Kennedy had just urged all Americans to build bomb shelters. A few years prior, Waco was hit by the deadliest tornado in American history. These people lived with ambient fear.

Cool rationalism might have analyzed the situation and realized a midsized town in Texas need not take the same precautions as residents in the Capitol, but reason rarely triumphs over emotion in troubled times. Intuition does not form in a vacuum, and the public fear caused smart people to react in illogical ways.

This prompts the question, what intuition do we now hold that may be the product of the emotion of our day? Consider your default reactions: What's happening to our nation? How do you view Evangelicals? Catholics? Liberals? Conservatives? Socialists? For many, one of these questions will provoke emotion. Why is that? Have you ever paused to question your intuition?

For some, it's a personal experience projected onto an entire segment of the population. Perhaps your childhood church was controlling, but does that mean all churches are controlling? You may intellectually recognize your experience is not a fair assessment of all Christians, but it's still your default reaction when you think of Evangelicals.

For others, their emotion stems from the common narrative surrounding a particular group. *All socialists are lazy. All conservatives are racists. All Evangelicals are legalistic.* Typically, these views result from a lack of exposure. You see it through the lens of history, news, and the opinions of others. Social media reinforces whatever we already believe, and the result can be a well-sealed echo chamber.

If your view of history is one-sided, or if you buy into an incomplete narrative, it will skew everything else. Things might seem obvious, common-sense, and intuitive to you, but that doesn't guarantee it's accurate. It may be the equivalent of building unnecessary bomb shelters. If we fail to pause for a moment to reflect on the source of our intuition, we may doom future generations to spend a day below ground, siphoning out the by-product of someone's irrational fear.

Secular Humanists routinely accuse believers of being narrow-minded, of refusing to confront our history and the difficult questions of our faith. It is especially common on college campuses and has created a narrative that Christians aren't intellectual. I've seen it explicitly stated that society shouldn't consider the perspective of believers because science has already proved us wrong on our beliefs.

Most secularists do not hold such overtly arrogant views, but they are still emotionally impacted by the narrative. I'm not sure they're aware of where it came from nor how it continues to shape the worldview clash.

Of course, this goes both ways. I'm troubled by the revisionist history some Christians teach, so I'm grateful for the wide range of Christian leaders who work hard to help the Church confront the sin of our past and expose our wrong viewpoints. However, I also believe Humanists are guilty of twisting history to reinforce their views, but I don't see much self-awareness or willingness to question their prevailing dogma.

We all see the world through a narrative, but few people take time to analyze the source of their perspective. I believe the old adage that victors write the history books. It's why Rome is good, and Carthage is bad. Centuries pass before historians start to question the claims of conquers, and often to mixed results. Myths endure long after being disproven.

I believe our attempt to understand worldview is largely shaped by flawed history, one written by the conquerors. Hundreds of years ago, Humanist scholars rewrote history to discredit the church and accuse Christians of being anti-science and anti-reason. This common narrative still sets the background noise in our quest to understand culture. It's like music playing in a store; you rarely pause to listen, but it still affects the atmosphere.

It's tragically ironic to see intellectuals perpetuate the myth that Christians are not intellectual. It would only take a little research to discover the vast contributions of believers to science, both past and present, but to do so would upset the narrative of a conflict between faith and reason. Many secularists rely on this to uphold their sense of moral superiority.

I believe both Humanism and the Kingdom require a faith science cannot fully prove. Both groups make assumptions about human nature, God, and our existence. These beliefs form a filter by which we interpret everything else.

I challenge anyone who tends toward a Humanist perspective to do their own research. I predict you'll find a lot of "facts" to be less clear than you think.

Most of us seldom think about worldview to begin with. If it ever crosses our mind, we don't analyze the origins of our perspective. I recognize you may not have thought about history since you left high school, and maybe you didn't even pay attention then. Bear with me for a chapter. No matter how irrelevant it may seem, our view of the past is the lens by which we view the present. Even if you don't study history, your viewpoints are still shaped by the way you understand it, and that is probably affecting the way you view culture.

THE FLAWED STORY OF HUMANISM

The secular perspective reads something like this: In the Dark Ages, a powerful Catholic church ruled with an iron fist and suppressed attempts at science, education, and equality. Mankind had rapidly advanced under Greek and Roman rule during the prior millennia, with an expansion of architecture, philosophy, arts, and government, but this human progress was abruptly stunted when the Roman Empire collapsed. It suspiciously coincided with the rise of Christianity and led Europe into a thousand years of darkness.

The power of the church increased during the period when barbarians invaded and destroyed civilization. The famous historian Edward Gibbons saw the rise of Christianity as a primary cause for Rome's decline. Libraries burned, knowledge vanished, and a brutal theocracy filled the power vacuum. Church doctrine prohibited science, economics, and exploration. Inquisitions suppressed any attempts to break off the clerical power. This stranglehold suppressed advancement for centuries.

But after a long sleep, agnostic scientists emerged and started to oppose the church; it all began with rediscovering ancient Greek texts. These brave souls placed reason above theology, rediscovered philosophy, and ushered in a new Age of Enlightenment. It was like rays of light piercing through the cultural darkness.

As intellectuals broke free from their religious chains, they led humanity into an unprecedented era of prosperity and peace, guided by reason alone. With each passing generation, religion grew less relevant and humanity progressed. Smart people saw no need for faith, leaving it as a crux for the weak and uneducated masses.

Charles Darwin drove the final nail into the coffin of faith, freeing people once and for all to leave behind their antiquated beliefs. The scientific and economic progress of the Enlightenment decisively proved the power of reason over faith. Religious belief was implied to be unintellectual, a sentimental relic of a past era.

"Religion is the opium of the people," remarked Karl Marx. Voltaire and others assumed religion would fade into obscurity. Nietzsche declared that, "God is dead." A claim still resurrected every few decades.

The underlying assumption in these famous perspectives is that reason and science stand at odds with religion. It teaches that these opposing camps have warred for hundred years, but reason has finally won, especially in the West. People may hold onto their beliefs, but eventually progress will triumph. Science will render religion irrelevant and, once freed, people will embrace Humanism and usher in an era of even greater advancement.

Our historical understanding shapes our perspective and influences the way we view culture. It affects our arguments and emotional reactions to faith. I believe it continues to frame the current conversation. It's why many Christians only feel ashamed by the history of the Church. It's why Secularists do not feel the need to seriously listen to the concerns of believers. If the Church is the villain of history, then our beliefs should be defeated, not accommodated.

If you feel a strong emotional reaction against a person or group, it is very difficult to interpret them objectively. It's called bias, and it affects everyone regardless of their intelligence. The philosopher Charles Taylor speaks of the "unthoughts" of modern intellectuals, describing it as the background belief shaping the way they view their discipline, saying:

> There is indeed a powerful such unthought operative: An outlook which holds that religion must decline either because it is false, and science shows this to be so; or because it is now increasingly irrelevant ... Indeed [this] is often part of the unnoticed background of social science, history, philosophy, psychology.[27]

Everyone likes to think of themselves as neutral, but we cannot separate ourselves from an unconscious bias, even when writing a history book or teaching a philosophy class. I'm not accusing people of malicious intent. By its very definition, unconscious means we don't realize we're doing it. This is the hidden power of the background noise and why history is important.

I believe well-meaning intellectuals created a culture which views religion with suspicion, smugly holding that faith is the province of the uneducated. If you believe this, then freeing people from their religious bonds emerges as a moral responsibility. You essentially become an evangelist of secularism.

These same people see Humanism as our natural mode. It's considered our default morality; at least once corrupted religious power is removed. Taylor calls this a subtraction theory, stating, "Once the old religious beliefs withered away, room was finally made for the existing, purely human moral motivation." In other words, Humanism itself is neutral and emerges organically once religion is disproven.

If you accept this story, Humanism takes on a type of Manifest Destiny. It allows you to make the claim that you stand on the right side of history. Our generation is seen as merely another chapter in a long-term struggle. Religion is the negative agent affecting the world; while Humanism leads to the freedom we all crave. People like to be on the winning team. Victors write the history books.

This is an evocative story. It's not a mere factual recounting of history; instead, it's framed as an epic struggle for liberation and, if you believe it, holds profound implications for worldview. I believe this narrative has a massive impact on how many people view the church, even Christians. How much does it affect you?

CHALLENGING THE NARRATIVE

But the whole narrative is largely inaccurate and incomplete. Much of the history we take for granted is controversial at best, parts are easily disproven, and the rest is more complicated than we realize. Academics can, and will, dispute individual points. I'm not qualified to make definitive judgments, but I do believe we need to challenge the narrative and stop giving it free reign to shape the way we view the world.

Charles Taylor and Rodney Stark each provide a much more thorough analysis on how we got to this point and I've drawn from both of their works throughout this chapter.

For starters, there was not a Dark Age; or if there was, it was much earlier. To have an Enlightenment, things first need to be dark and then become light. That's not to say there weren't problems. Pick a century in world history and you'll find violence, calamity, and oppression—including our own. But the idea of agnostic scholars rescuing the world from a thousand years of darkness is wrong.

The twin blows of the Black Death and the Hundred Years' War in the fourteenth century was a near unprecedented tragedy. Globally, the population declined by twenty-five percent; in Europe it was closer to fifty. This certainly was a time of darkness, but not one caused by the church. Under Catholic leadership, humanity rapidly advanced in the centuries prior to this destruction; once the dust settled a few hundred years later, progress once again continued, just under different leadership.

Many "Enlightenment" philosophers revered the mighty Roman Empire and considered it a high point of human achievement. After all, Romans built a transportation network, large cities, and grand buildings. But these scholars fail to mention that it was all built on the backs of slaves, who accounted for half the population. The longevity of its reign was impressive, but that doesn't signify human progress. For most of the population it was brutal tyranny. Was Rome's collapse a tragedy? Or freedom? I guess it depends on who you ask.

James Franklin, professor at University of New South Wales, does identify a Dark Ages but places it in the five hundred years following Rome's collapse. Stark views the disintegrating Empire as the catalyst for innovation. Either way, history refutes the common story of a dark world held back solely by an oppressive church.

To summarize Stark, during these "dark ages," universities formed, technological improvements reshaped most aspects of life, new science evolved our understanding of the world, and capitalism was birthed—all under the leadership of the church. "Enlightenment" philosophers took credit for these previous innovations, added some ideas of their own, and then claimed to lead the world out of the darkness. These men even coined the term "Enlightenment" to describe their own work, disregarding the contributions of previous generations. The arrogance is rather striking.

Stark goes on to state:

The single most remarkable and ironic thing about the "Enlightenment" is that those who proclaimed it made little or no contribution to the accomplishments they hailed as a revolution in human knowledge, while those responsible for these advances stressed continuity with the past.[31]

Once the "Enlightenment" began, much of the progress was led by devout Christians. I've already mentioned William Wilberforce and slavery as an example, but that's just the beginning. Much of the educational and medical system was pioneered by strong Christians, whose primary motivation was the Kingdom. This led them to sacrificially serve neglected people. The same can be said for humanitarian relief and ministry to the poor.[32]

Over time, some of these institutions drifted toward secularism, but Christians continue to pioneer and lead. Secular Humanism cannot take credit for social consciousness and charity. I'm glad they embrace the same ideals but challenge them to remember that they owe their very existence to Christian theology and practice. This is conveniently left out of the narrative. Pesky facts ruin good stories.

I certainly don't agree with much of the theology nor the practice of the Medieval Catholic church. The church did oppress some scientists and commit horrific injustice toward minority groups. The era around and after the Reformation saw particularly violent religious conflict. I'm not arguing that this time was peaceful nor that the church was advancing the Kingdom, but I'm unwilling to buy the "Humanism saved the world from religion" version either. Like most things, reality is more nuanced.

People find themselves resisting faith because to them it's a sign of intellectual weakness or, even worse, a barrier to progress. But much of this is an emotional reaction based on flawed understanding. I find it rather hypocritical to accuse Christians of ignorance and bias only to be guilty of the same.

HUMANISM'S ORIGINS

Like the historical narrative, the belief that Humanism is our default morality is also deeply flawed. It is not some neutral worldview that inevitably emerged when religion faded. As we saw in Chapter 3, Humanism is an active belief system. It originated in the same way as any other sect, even though it's non-religious.

Charles Taylor goes to great lengths to chart its emergence in his book *A Secular Age*. He saw Humanism's early development take place amongst devout Christians. These foundational concepts weren't challenges to the Church; they emerged from within it. Three biblical ideas created the environment for Secular Humanism's later emergence.

First, Christians started to focus on the humanity of Jesus and, in the process, emphasized our own humanity. They still held a high view of God, but also began to explore how God sees us. This sparked the rise of individualism.

Second, many believers theorized that if God created the world, and if He is a God of order, then His order can be known.

This led them to search out the laws of God, later known as natural laws. This contrasted with the fatalistic viewpoints of previous generations, as well as other leading religions, which viewed God as unknowable. These new theories created the environment for modern science to emerge.

Individualism and science combined to empower men and women to shape the world in radically new ways. People no longer lived at the mercy of gods and spirits, but instead were empowered by God to transform their world and their lives. This birthed the Protestant work ethic and the critical mindsets required for Secular Humanism to develop.

Lastly, the church emphasized the need for reform, leading to a focus on educating the masses as well as improving morality within believers. The Reformation and its counter fueled the fire. Over time, a moral code developed and was even prioritized over faith. This eventually allowed Humanism to shed religious belief while still maintaining social order.

As the theologian Craig Gay notes, "It was within our own Western tradition – and due almost entirely to the impact of the Christian religion within it – that the concerns for authentic individuality and for the infinite value of the human person developed." Max Weber famously recognized the role of the Christian faith on modern life as the basis for his Protestant Work Ethic thesis.

Os Guinness says it this way, "The Christian faith contributed decisively to the rise of the modern world, but it has been undermined decisively by the modern world it helped to create. The Christian faith has become its own gravedigger."[34]

It was the violent Thirty Years' War that shocked the intellectual elites of Europe and caused them to rethink their religious views. Not a mass falling away from the faith, but rather a slow drift. They saw the danger of religious enthusiasm first hand and decided to de-emphasize doctrine to avoid future conflicts. Over time, the name *Deism* defined the new perspective.

Deism was the midpoint between Medieval Christianity and Secular Humanism. This belief system held that there is a God who upholds a moral code to which we will be held accountable, but that the doctrine of the various denominations does not necessarily reflect the Creator. Deists focused on morality and called people to live according to the natural laws established by the Creator God. God was removed from daily activity in this world, and our primary interaction with Him was through His created order. As a result, grace was de-emphasized.

With the passing of each new century, philosophers gradually shed religious beliefs and the corresponding moral codes. Our modern worldview was first theorized by the likes of John Stuart Mill and Virginia Woolf. It's only been in the last generation that their ideas have fully bloomed to truly shape society.

Proponents of Humanism may view their belief as the default philosophy once religion is removed, but their entire worldview was powerfully shaped by the Christian faith and developed in much the same way as a religious sect. It's not our "natural" worldview; instead, it's something carefully taught and disciplined into our culture.

Like all belief systems, Humanism strives to convert people and change culture. It's active and has an agenda. It also has similar problems to religion. At times, Humanism shows intolerance and continues to teach revisionist history to validate its worldviews.

I'm not excusing the many ways the Church has done the same, but I'm also unwilling to accept Humanist claims to serve as our definitive moral code. I see many Christians apologizing for not conforming to Humanism's morality. They seem to believe our faith should submit to the authority of this "natural" ethical system. I'm all for repenting for the sins of our past, but I'm not converting to Humanism. I don't believe it's going to work; I don't buy into its narrative; and I have no plans to submit to its worldview.

IT'S NOT ALL BAD

Despite my concerns, I want to reiterate a point I made earlier in the book: I agree with most of Humanism's morality—especially considering it's based on the teachings of Jesus, even if they fail to give Him credit. I think the focus on human development over the last five hundred years transformed the world in positive ways.

Fatalistic, religious worldviews ruled the time prior to Humanism's development. This was not limited to Christianity. Across the world, religion taught that we were powerless and at the mercy of various gods and spirits. This kept people trapped in ignorance and injustice, and you can still find it in our world today.

I once traveled with a humanitarian organization to a North African nation embroiled in a bloody civil war. Every night I fell asleep to gunfire, but not the sound of fighting. The front lines were miles away. This was the sound of celebration. "Martyrs" were celebrated by shooting guns in the air. Victories were pronounced by the same method. I think some of the fire was just for fun. In my humble opinion, this method was rather short-sighted. What goes up must come down, and my calculations told me to stay clear of windows.

It seems obvious this was all one bad idea, but it originated in the culture's fatalistic view of God. They shot guns into the air without regard for where the bullets fell. To them, if someone was accidentally killed then it was God's will, which absolved the shooters of responsibility. Many innocent people died, apparently because God willed it.

Early Humanism helped balance out this type of perspective. It taught us that God empowered us to take responsibility. Modern science and the other innovative ideas which emerged out of the Middle Ages are not the problem; I certainly don't want to return to the Medieval period.

Humanity has advanced in incredible ways in the last five hundred years. Christians and Humanists both deserve credit for the positive, and both deserve blame for the negative. They also share a lot of common ground.

Each of these worldviews teach us to prioritize discipline, responsibility, and innovation. We also agree on our social responsibility. We agree in the belief that every person on this planet holds intrinsic value and should be celebrated and cared for. These beliefs may seem obvious, but this is a minority view across human history, perhaps even still to this day. I find a lot of common ground with Humanists. I also recognize they've helped point out hypocrisy in the Church, and for that I'm grateful.

Once we reset the narrative, we can approach the conversation with a more balanced perspective. I don't believe the Humanist narrative nor accept their worldview, but I can appreciate our common beliefs. These overlapping values allows us to discover plenty of places to partner. I reject the pressure to conform; and in so doing, I don't feel the need to reject the people with whom I disagree. Appreciating our distinctions will help the relationship.

Be confident in your faith. Don't allow the intensity of our culture to pull you away. As you do, I believe you'll find fresh grace to relate to people on the other side of the aisle.

CHAPTER 6

VIEWS OF MORALITY

Many Christians mistakenly believe our society is becoming amoral. "There are no more standards for right living." "No one cares about right and wrong." I hear this a lot from believers as they seek to understand a culture that appears to have lost all sense of morality.

However, I believe the exact opposite is happening. Our nation is intensely moral, even fundamentalist, but we disagree on what is right. The competing versions of morality cause us to misdiagnose our culture. Humanists are equally as rigid as their Christian neighbors, just with a different focus.

THE NEW MORAL MAJORITY

"Chick-Fil-A's Creepy Infiltration of New York City" is the title of an article published by *The New Yorker* magazine. It views the fast food chain's rapid expansion in the city as a threat to culture. The issue of national brands overrunning local restaurants is of secondary concern. Its author probed deeper to highlight a more sinister menace, stating, "The brand's arrival here feels like an infiltration, in no small part because of its pervasive Christian traditionalism."[35]

Plenty of other chains entered the city without disturbing the palace guards. Many of these corporations take a strong stance on social issues but avoid scrutiny because they fit the Humanist culture. Not Chick-Fil-A and its Christian heritage. Mayor Bill de Blasio encouraged New Yorkers to avoid the brand. City Council member Christine Quinn publicly proclaimed the chain was not welcome in the city. Protesters greeted the arrival of the first location.

It all reminds me of the heyday of the Christian Right. It's the same tactics, just a different side. Cultured New Yorkers fear Evangelicals inserting their troubling beliefs into the city much in the same way that southern Evangelicals feared a secret Satanist group meeting underneath the Capitol building.

In the 1980s, Clorox, Burger King, and other companies were boycotted by religious groups because their television commercials aired on programs that conflicted with Christian values. The tactic used public opinion to limit the spread of immoral values. Now this method is used against Evangelicals for the exact same reason.

These attempts try to force companies into an active role in policing morality. None of the boycotts were in relation to a company product or policy. Clorox wasn't dealing drugs nor was Chick-Fil-A discriminating. The culprit stemmed from things like the founders' private comments, political donations, and advertising partnerships. It's a culture war, and the combatants are willing to conscript just about anyone.

I'm not trying to address concerns of free expression, nor a company's moral responsibility, nor any of the other issues related to these examples; instead my goal is to point out the intense moral environment we live in. One wrong statement can cost you a job—this doesn't happen in an amoral society. One slightly controversial post can end a friendship. The very act of writing this book might limit my future opportunities in certain fields. Our society is very concerned with right and wrong, just not as defined in Scripture.

When surrounded by opposing views of morality, it's easy to spend time reacting. At times this may be outrage, while at other times it may be defensive. If we aren't careful, responding to the intensity of our culture will overshadow our mission. Believers cannot allow Humanism or Cultural Christianity to define how we live.

The cultural power of Christianity is waning while the power of Humanism ascends. We're not leaving behind the era of the Moral Majority; we're trading it in for a new one. Cultural Christianity still has teeth in certain locations, but Humanism is stronger. Our society has a fundamentalist streak—just not necessarily religious—and many of us live caught between the opposing poles.

The goal of any fundamentalist group is rigid adherence to a moral code. Once a group secures enough power, they generally attempt to enforce their rules across society, whether you believe or not. This is accomplished through boycotts, legal regulations, public shaming, ideological purity tests, and guilt-by-association accusations.

The threat of being outed forces opponents into silence and provides the illusion of conformity. Thirty years ago, a devout atheist needed to suppress their beliefs to advance in society. Today the same atheist is freer to live openly, while a professing Evangelical may discover a greater social cost to publicly express his or her faith. There are many variables to this—industry, geography, and more. I don't intend it as a blanket statement. An atheist running for office will still face immense hurdles in the Deep South, but the trend is pointing the other way.

George Yancey is a sociologist who has specialized in studying both racial bias and religious bias in the United States. His research revealed that overall hostility toward Evangelicals has not increased in recent decades, but it has shifted to wealthier and more influential detractors.[36] In other words, people with the power to shape culture are increasingly antagonistic toward believers. Active Christians have always been a minority, but in eras past we held considerable social power. This is diminishing.

It is perhaps most evident in higher education. "Speech violence" is an extreme example of this phenomenon. The basic principle holds that words cause stress and stress causes bodily harm; therefore, certain types of speech are a form of violence. This is the pretext used by campus activists to prevent opposing viewpoints from finding a place, often by any means necessary. Rather than debating divergent views, conflicting opinions are forcefully suppressed.

This stance is controversial among liberals and conservatives alike,[37] and is generally limited to areas of race relations. However, its influence is still broadly felt. Christian student groups have been kicked off campus for requiring members to adhere to Christian beliefs. Professors and graduate students are less likely to be hired simply because they have traditional Christian beliefs.[38] In other words, Christians are not tolerated because they believe in Christianity. Religious beliefs must conform to Humanist beliefs or they will be considered bigoted and potentially dangerous. Christian ethics are dangerous to non-believers and thus can be legitimately suppressed.

Humans have long sought to silence views that made them uncomfortable and invented a wide range of excuses to do so—heresy, public safety, and more. "Speech violence" is new clothing for an ancient ploy—one the Church is just as guilty of as anyone else.

To be clear, I do not believe Christians are being persecuted in America. I've seen real persecution, and this isn't it. Secondly, most Humanists are not fundamentalist, much in the same way that most Christians aren't either.

Extreme positions hold a lot of power because average people fear standing up to them. In modern America, people fear being labeled a bigot, so they stay silent even when they disagree with activists trying to suppress viewpoints. No one likes to be a heretic.

It is not easy to live as a minority in a society that is seeking to impose a rigid moral code, but this is our new environment. We need to prepare churches for this era. It will require language to discuss our differences. We'll need to intensify our discipleship efforts, knowing we are up against a strong current. At times, we may need to publicly take a stand on topics that will cost us.

FUNDAMENTALISM'S FLAW

Despite the challenges, I'm not worried. Fundamentalism has a poor track record. It cannot deliver on cultural change because its power is limited to external conformity. People eventually grow weary of thought-police and the never-ending quest for more ideological purity. No matter how much you conform, it's never enough—an emotional black hole always demanding more.

Additionally, hypocrisy always lurks in the shadows of fundamentalism. This doomed the Moral Majority in the 1980s. Jimmy Swaggart was a prominent televangelist who preached against the influences of immorality in culture, even exposing the sin of other pastors. His fame spread for years, until he was photographed entering a motel room with a prostitute in Louisiana. He repented, only to get caught with a different prostitute in California. He was certainly not the only Christian leader to suffer this fate.

But duplicity is not unique to the religious right. In recent years, sexual harassment accusations have toppled many of Hollywood's most influential. The televangelists of Humanism have their own hypocrisy problem.

Talk show superstar Matt Lauer lost his job for sexual misconduct. This happened shortly after his moralizing attack on another media personality who was fired for the same offense. Harvey Weinstein shaped Hollywood and much of its sexual ethics for decades. He contributed to social causes and claimed to advance women's rights. But it all came crashing down after a *New York Times* exposé revealed a horrific career of sexual abuse.

I pray the increased scrutiny leads to genuine change. I also sincerely hope that exposing hypocrisy will provoke us all to look in the mirror. However, I am concerned with how easily we find ourselves swept up by the intensity of our culture without stopping to consider the underlying worldview.

It's easy to get outraged over a legitimate problem in society and show solidarity with fellow citizens to demand change. I believe believers need to confront injustice, but I find many take it further and soon begin to embrace the whole moral system. Sometimes it aligns with the faith while, at others, it opposes the Kingdom worldview. If we aren't careful, our allegiance subtly transfers to Humanism. Many of us have no clue we are doing it.

The current Humanist climate strives to hold everyone accountable to standards they cannot keep themselves. For the record, I wholeheartedly believe in most of the standards—sexual harassment of any form is incredibly wrong, as is discrimination, systemic racism, and many other modern ails. But I don't think the approach is working. We can scapegoat a few people all we want, but the root issue is not just them, it's all of us.

Fundamentalism doesn't work. Forced morality has very little power because it cannot change human nature. Disillusionment always follows in its wake.

THE RADICAL KINGDOM

Culture wars hide the real problem. We spend so much time dodging bullets, sometimes from both sides, that we lose sight of our calling. The act of breathing and muttering a few words is probably enough to get you labeled a cultural heretic.

I feel pressure from both Cultural Christians and Humanists to conform and pick a side, but the Kingdom worldview leads us into an entirely different way of living. This is inherently uncomfortable. If we don't feel tension, it means we've conformed to something that's not the Kingdom. Not belonging to this world is a necessary aspect of walking with Jesus.

Jesus faced similar pressures from the competing worldviews of His day. The conservative Jews sought to co-opt Him into their cause of restoring a sovereign state, while the liberal elites tried to prove He was antagonistic to the Romans. Both sides attempted to use Him as a pawn in their geopolitical game.

He faced repeated trick questions attempting to force Him to pick a side. Rather than conform, He preached a Kingdom message that offended both parties. When He refused to acquiesce to either of the worldviews, the two opponents united to oppose Him.

On one occasion, a religious expert was sent to test Him with a complex question: "What is the most important of God's commands?"

Jesus replied: "'Love the Lord your God with all your heart and with all your soul and with all your mind.' This is the first and greatest commandment. And the second is like it: 'Love your neighbor as yourself.' All the Law and the Prophets hang on these two commandments." Matthew 22:37-39

Jesus used the trap to pronounce the foundational ethic of the Kingdom worldview: A love for God and a love for people. It's that simple, and it's that radical. This matters more than nationalism. It's more important than forcing people to live according to a moral code.

The emphasis is not behavioral change. The Kingdom teaches that everything must flow from a transformed heart. If you truly love God and love people, your behavior will certainly change, but the focus is no longer on self.

The message of Jesus holds a completely different focus from our modern viewpoints. Both Humanism and Cultural Christianity are fundamentally based on us. They appear different on the surface but stem from the same foundation, which holds that the key to thriving is found within me. This takes on different approaches: On the one side, it looks like conforming to a moral code through my own effort. On the other, it teaches me to maximize my happiness and live true to my dreams. But they both start by placing self at the center.

The Kingdom provides an entirely different way of viewing the world. How would you live if you were not at the center of your life? Can you even visualize what this looks like? We're so conditioned to focus on ourselves—our reputation, dreams, and happiness—it's difficult to consider a life focused on others.

The grace of God and sacrificial love anchors the Kingdom worldview. We cede control over our happiness and self-worth, and instead find fulfillment in God. He gives us identity, He leads us into joy and peace, and He empowers us to love others.

Sacrificial love is the core difference between the Kingdom and all other perspectives. If my life is based on myself, I will not lay down my life for others. I may seek to be good, I may have close relationships, but I won't truly sacrifice. By contrast, the Kingdom originates within the sacrificial love of Jesus, which then transforms us, so we can sacrificially love others. Humanism teaches us to do no harm and strive to be good to others. The Kingdom calls us to lay down our life.

Love frees me to stop focusing on me. My identity is not shaped by sexuality, or material wealth, or cultural power, or religious superiority. Instead, I'd freely surrender any of this if it hinders me from loving God and loving others. The world emphasizes those things as our ticket to fulfillment; the Kingdom teaches that we flourish in a relationship based on unconditional love.

I'm not talking about a martyr mentality, which equates unhappiness with holiness. I believe God wants us to thrive and enjoy this life, but this only happens when we walk in close relationship with Him. Sex is a wonderful gift within certain boundaries. Material possessions are a blessing but should never define us. Cultural influence can be a powerful tool but should never serve as our identity. The Kingdom is a paradox. By surrendering the things the world teaches will give us happiness, we find the joy and purpose we so desperately want.

Our culture teaches us to flourish in our own strength and our own abilities. It takes on a religious flavor for some and a worldly flavor for others; a lot of people swing back-and-forth between both. Neither satisfy. The way up is down. The way to life is by embracing death.

Walking with Jesus is an act of faith. We're choosing to surrender our desires and instead trust Him to meet our needs. It's vulnerable but isn't that the whole point of love? My life is scarred by sin. It wages war against me and will destroy me if left unchecked, but it provides an illusion of control and happiness. That's why it's so difficult to let go. It's only grace that sets us free.

A NEW WAY FORWARD

The pressure of fundamentalism on either side causes us to lose sight of this foundation of love. To fully live the second greatest commandment, I believe we must start by living the first. Rigidly following a few of the Bible's commands is useless if it's not based in love.

This applies on an individual level as well as the societal. If the heart is not transformed, no amount of restored cultural power will save Christianity. Regaining political clout does not advance the Kingdom. Saying "Merry Christmas" again is not very helpful if people don't know the Christ.

I still believe the extent to which a culture follows God's ways is the extent to which it will thrive. I'd certainly prefer our nation's moral code to be based on the commands of God. Politics has its place, as does activism, but they shouldn't be in the driver seat. The whole story of the Old Testament proves His standards are unattainable unless our hearts are transformed by the Gospel.

Our nation is intensely moral, and the culture wars show no sign of slowing down. New fronts emerge to expand the battle across every part of our society, affecting everything from education, to sports, to history, to family life, and to politics. Sometimes the battle is based on religious practices while at other times it's purely cultural. This environment is difficult to navigate in our quest to follow Jesus.

The question of when and how to engage on individual topics is complex. The next section of this book will evaluate several of what I consider to be the most prominent places of divergence between Humanism and the Kingdom. These represent issues where those following a Humanist ethic will reach a different conclusion than those following the Kingdom.

As we discuss distinct topics, I do believe there are times we need to speak out on hot-button issues. Some of these have major implications and will affect the world for years to come. I'm not trying to minimize their importance. But, before we wade into the details, I think it's important to ask a bigger question: How do we keep the focus on the love of God?

Let's not let someone else's fundamentalism define us. They may have valid points; they may point out legitimate problems in our society. I find myself agreeing with Cultural Christianity on some issues and Humanists on others, but I don't want to conform to the underlying spirit of our age.

I wholly recognize no one completely lives within the Kingdom worldview. We live in the Now of God's Kingdom, but the Not Yet of seeing its full manifestation. Grace is alive and well, but this side of Heaven we still wrestle with the lingering stain of sin. I'm not claiming to live completely from a Gospel-centered perspective, but this is my goal. As much as possible in this life, let's press into it.

It's easy to get cynical when dealing with people, and this often causes us to lose our ideals. This is why the Gospel is so important; my faith must be in Jesus, not people. A right foundation allows me to love broken people, because they do not define me. It's tragic when Christians hurt others through their sin, but this does not invalidate the person of Jesus. I'd rather contend for the Kingdom, knowing I'll fall short, then give up and acquiesce to the sin of our world.

The world is desperate for genuine love and peace. People are tired of the constant bickering and power plays. What a tragedy if we get sucked into the wrong battle, especially when we hold the solution the world so anxiously seeks.

When everyone else is flinging insults online and projecting their own discontentment onto national politics, I pray the Church rediscovers the power of what we do best—loving God wholeheartedly, sacrificially loving our neighbors, and serving the needs of our community. This may go unrecognized on a cultural level, at least for a while, but it's the substance of what people crave. It's what we've been freely given by grace, and therefore freely give away.

I want my attention transfixed on the radical love of Jesus. I want Him to shape the way I view problems in society. I want Him to shape the way I view people. Ultimately, I want Him to shape the way I view myself. Though I fall woefully short, this remains my goal. When His grace defines my worldview, I find everything else falls into place. No matter how complex the social issue, if we start here then we'll find the right path.

CHAPTER 7

SEXUAL MORALS AND INTIMACY

The earth groaned beneath Mary Wambui as she sat to eat dinner with her family. It felt like some biblical plague when a sudden crack split the ground under her feet and continued until it tore the house in two. The tear continued for kilometers, growing into a fifty-foot deep rift that cut through farmland and across a busy highway.

Geologists say this is only the beginning for Kenya's Narok County. East Africa is slowly forming into a new continent, and this new tear represents the latest boundary. A series of narrow lakes already form a broken line extending more than a thousand miles. New rifts will form, and existing ones will expand. Mary's living room will ultimately rest at the bottom of the ocean floor.

This dramatic event startled the country, but for most of life, the monumental change occurs unseen. The occasional fissure is a mere symptom of a much greater reality, and it's a fitting illustration to describe our worldview transformation. In some aspects of culture, the change is imperceptible, at least for now. But other issues provide a dramatic example of what is taking place under our feet.

Many people feel the ground splitting underneath them. For some, their home was split in two as family members now hold to a different moral code. The gap only widens with each passing year. Sexual morals form the most obvious rift between the Humanist and Kingdom worldviews. We'll look at other differences in future chapters, but this is the most glaring. How we experience sex, love, and relationships stand at ground zero in the worldview clash.

Before we analyze this topic, think back to the cultural stronghold that shapes your thinking. This profoundly impacts the way you view intimacy. I'm using multiple words to describe this topic because, though our perspective on sex is the most obvious, I believe the issue is broader and affects our deepest relationships and our view of love itself.

My basic premise is that a large percentage of Christians today adhere to orthodox theology but emotionally live as Humanists. As a result, we feel deep tension around sexuality because our emotions conflict with our beliefs. The biblical perspective on sex stands as a barrier to the ideals of modern culture. Much of our world views Christian teaching as a type of Victorian-era relic holding people back from experiencing a full life.

While Humanism influences more Christians, some believers may still be shaped by Cultural Christianity in their view of sex. On the surface, this appears to closely agree with the Kingdom; however, the alignment is deceptive. They might agree on right behaviors, but the motivations differ. The distinction is harder to see.

The intensity of the differences on this topic generates a wide range of debate and often erupts into political conversations. What is the purpose of marriage? What role does sex play in human fulfillment? What moral restrictions are simply remnants of the past? We spend a lot of time arguing these points, but our perspective originates from our underlying worldview.

I will not agree on sexual morals with a Secular Humanist no matter how much we talk. My whole belief system takes me in a different direction than theirs.

Countless books, sermons, and articles address virtually every subject related to intimacy. I will not attempt to address the complexity of these issues, especially in just one chapter. Instead, my goal is to highlight how our default worldview affects the way we view the topic. This is the lens by which we view everything else. It may not answer the questions, but it determines the way we approach them.

The intensity of our sexual charged culture prompts a lot of backlash from believers, and rightfully so, but I fear we spend so much time reacting against the world that we lose sight of God's intention for intimate relationships. Before we spend time responding to the modern rift, we need to rediscover the beauty of Jesus' love. I believe once we see Him clearly, it will put everything else into focus.

THE KINGDOM PERSPECTIVE

Sacrificial love shapes the Kingdom worldview; it's the ultimate moral and shapes our understanding of the Bible's view of intimacy. Jesus modeled this with His very life. Words alone could never suffice to explain His love, so He stepped into our world to demonstrate it.

Love cost Him dearly. He embraced the life of a nomad and gave up His comforts to serve the marginalized. Jesus was misunderstood and betrayed—often by the same people He care for the most. But He never quit. Love caused Him to endure a crown of thorns. Love prompted Him to take up a cross and die the death of a traitor. This was no accident. Jesus chose His fate, and He did it for us.

Jesus lived unstained by sin, and therefore He loved with complete purity. Unfortunately, our love is not, and therein lies the problem. Our love is tainted with selfishness, forcing us to question to what extent we can love sacrificially in this life. Is it possible? Modern culture takes a different path, asking if this is even the right goal in the first place. Humanism suggests a new approach by encouraging us to focus on meeting our own needs in a way that leads to mutual benefit with others.

Despite our inherent sinfulness, the Bible is clear on how we should live. The Great Commandment calls believers to love God and love each other. The Greek word "agape" is translated into the English word "love," but no word quite captures the concept. It's unlike the type of love taught in modern culture. We use the same word, but with a different meaning.

We say, "I loved a movie," or "I loved a show," using the same English word to describe Jesus dying on a cross to redeem humanity. I'm no linguist, but this seems problematic. First century believers ran into the same problem. *Agape* was rarely used prior to the Scriptures; it was as though it was chosen because all existing words proved insufficient to describe the love of God. You cannot understand the Gospel apart from it.

This love lays down its life; this love gives up a one and only Son; this love covers the stains of sin; this love keeps no record of wrongs. It always protects, always trusts, always hopes, always perseveres. This love should be the driving force behind our relationships, and none more so than marriage.

Christian marriages are based on the love of Christ. The Apostle Paul wrote, "Husbands, love your wives, just as Christ loved the church and gave himself up for her ... 'For this reason a man will leave his father and mother and be united to his wife, and the two will become one flesh.' This is a profound mystery—but I am talking about Christ and the church. "

God intended the marriage relationship to model His love—one built on mutual submission and sacrifice. Sex is the physical representation of this intimacy. In the creation story, Adam's loneliness was the only thing in the Garden that God declared was "not good." Marriage and sex were instituted before sin—a beautiful, pleasurable, and holy thing that, in the right context, reveals to us the love of God.

But sin distorted our view of sex and warped our closest relationships. Sexual intimacy is incredibly powerful: Sex creates new life; marriage and parenting display the sacrificial love of Jesus; and intimacy is one of the greatest longings of the human heart. Woven together, these images form a powerful display, possessing immense potential to shape our lives.

Intimacy is the source of our highest joy and our greatest brokenness. When exercised rightly, it meets our deep needs and provides an environment to flourish and see the love of God revealed to us through human interaction. When this power is used poorly, or abused, people experience profound pain. In the very place God intended them to see His love most visibly, they instead feel the sting of sin.

The power of intimacy is why God instituted boundaries. No loving parent allows their toddler to play in a busy street, because they understand the fleeting joy is not worth the hazard. God likewise sought to protect us. Herein lies the rift: Modern culture views God's guidelines as a limitation to fullness, while the Kingdom teaches these exist to guard us.

The Bible clearly expresses God's standards, teaching us sex is reserved for the context of a life-long marriage between a man and a woman. Separating the thrill of intimacy from a commitment to sacrificial love leaves you with a cheap substitute. Infidelity, premarital sex, and pornography all represent a departure from God's design. No matter how good it feels, these will not lead to life.

In the Kingdom worldview, sexual intimacy beautifully represents the love of God, but only when expressed within His boundaries. Upholding this standard is costly. Though it may seem crazy to our modern culture, remember that anything of great value will come at a price. There is no other way.

THE PROBLEM OF COUNTERFEITS

Unfortunately, valuable things are susceptible to counterfeits. If the authentic is too expensive, then why not settle for a fake?

Forgery plagues the art world, with some estimating it affects over ten percent of all work displayed in major museums. The problem is so prevalent that the Museum of Art Fakes recently opened in Vienna to display prominent forgeries. The museum even claims to possess "faked fake paintings."

Few forgers match the celebrated fraud of Han van Meegeren. Several recent books highlight the career of the wartime Dutch painter who once sold a forged Dutch masterpiece to a Nazi general. After the war, prosecutors charged van Meegeren with treason for supplying the occupiers with priceless art. The sentence for treason was death, and the evidence overwhelming. Van Meegeren could only defend himself by revealing his fraud. But in a comedic twist, the Dutch loved the prospective of cheating the Nazis and let him off lightly; however, his deception unnerved the art world.

In writing about van Meegeren and the broader problem of forgery, art critic Peter Schjeldahl remarked that, "Faith in authorship matters. We read the qualities of a work as the forthright decisions of a particular mind, wanting to let it commandeer our own minds, and we are disappointed when it doesn't."[40]

Art is more than brush strokes. It reveals the creator's hand and with it their deepest thoughts. Forgeries reproduce the image at the expense of the heart. They look similar, but no longer expose the emotions of the artist. It's a cheap substitute and, once discovered, it loses its value.

Upon his exposure, van Meegeren was purported to have said, "Yesterday, this painting was worth millions and art lovers came from all over the world to pay money to see it. Today, it is worth nothing and nobody would cross the street to see it for free. But the picture has not changed. What has?"

I believe this is an analogy for our culture. The Creator reveals His heart to us through the love found in human relationships. When we sacrificially love a spouse in the context of marriage, and all this entails, including both the joy of sex and the endurance through suffering, then we see His hand. It provides us a glimpse of the nature of God, and we see beyond the confines of this world.

But agape love has been reduced to a forgery in our culture. The brush strokes may seem similar—sexual intimacy, marriage contracts, and the like—but its essence is missing. Sacrificial love costs everything. Modern culture "frees" us to experience sexual pleasure without paying the price. It may feel good for a moment, but this type of "love" is a mere shadow of what God intended.

Fighting against forgery is complicated, especially when involving our emotions. In the art world, scientific analysis and provenance are important tools to fight fraud, but technology alone is always insufficient, because it arms both the forger and the expert. New defenses are matched by even more sophisticated schemes. Instead, experts describe their familiarity, even intimacy, with an artist as the best defense against fakes. I believe the same holds true for believers.

Worldview is complicated, but our best response is quite simple: We need an active, deep, growing, and genuine relationship with Jesus. He must become our highest priority and greatest influence. His love must extend beyond a theoretical concept for us to truly understand.

Smart people still get taken in by clever ploys. This is the true brilliance of most forgers. They pray upon the emotions and the desires of their marks. If you truly analyzed what the world calls love and contrasted it to the love of God, then I believe the difference jumps out clearly. The problem is that the modern forgery fits the emotion of our culture, making it particularly deceptive.

Many Christians find themselves unwittingly deceived by this scheme. I believe we are swept up into our culture's entire worldview related to sex, love, and relationships. Like art fraud, our primary problem is a lack of intimacy with the Master. We don't truly know His work, so we can be duped by clever forgeries.

The degree to which we understand the depth of Christ's sacrificial love and grace is the degree to which we embrace His vision for our own intimate relationships. Once this is clear, we more easily discern the counterfeit.

COMPETING PERSPECTIVES ON INTIMACY

In our battle to regain God's design for sexual intimacy, we face the intense pressure of Humanism, while simultaneously grappling with the flawed legacy of Cultural Christianity. This worldview emphasized right conduct but often missed the underlying goal of agape love. When it came to external behavior, no moral was more important than sex.

Those who failed to maintain the standard often suffered a lifetime of shame and ostracization. Cultural Christianity sought to enforce behaviors apart from transforming grace. Sexual sin was the ultimate taboo, but cultural pressure cannot cure natural urges. As a result, sex went into hiding.

People cannot live according to God's standards in their own strength, so they covered up their sexual behavior. Outwardly, they put on a moral face, but life looked different behind closed doors. Shame ruled the day.

This is where Humanism stepped in with a series of blows directed against the traditional Christian ethic. No one really lives this standard, they declared, so let's stop pretending like we do. The sexual revolution promoted the concept of "free love," which sought to free sex from the confines of marriage. It questioned the wisdom behind biblical standards. Why stigmatize genetic desires? What makes it unclean? They saw no barrier other than a Christian morality that overstayed its welcome.

These philosophies weren't new, but the hippies broke it into the mainstream. In the decades prior to the 1960s, television reliably reinforced Christian moral teaching. Authority figures in media, school, and government toed the cultural line, even if they lived the opposite when they stepped outside the lights.

Today, our world looks much different. *The Leave It to Beaver* days are long gone. Now eighty percent of all major network television shows include sexual content. It's hard to escape it. Pornography graduated from seedy gas stations to iPhones, more than nine in ten boys will be exposed to it during adolescence, most without ever leaving their bedroom. More significantly, conventional wisdom doesn't even see this as a problem, with many voices saying pornography is a healthy part of sexual development.

Humanism does uphold its own sexual morals, primarily around the idea of consent. In the transition out of Cultural Christianity, a staggering amount of sexual abuse has been exposed. We learned this was rampant in homes, schools, and churches, even though society appeared moral on the outside. Most victims feared the shame associated with their abuse and kept quiet, often for decades.

Secularists view this as a repudiation of the Christian ethic. Cultural Christianity reinforced a standard people could not keep, which forced people into hiding and allowed an abusive environment to flourish. On this point, I agree. Morals without grace leads to hypocrisy.

But I disagree with the entire premise of the sexual revolution. There is no such thing as free love. This betrays the entire definition of agape. Reducing love to the physical act of sex is a terrible degradation of what God intended.

Believers often must choose between sex and love. To truly show love for God and people, there are many situations in which we must say no to sex. Single Christians forgo sexual pleasure to show their love for Jesus by obeying His boundaries. Married believers stay faithful to their spouse, rejecting any other form of sexual pleasure for the sake of love. Kingdom love involves sacrifice, including the right to sex.

Our culture cannot understand. If you believe that the highest goal in life is to be true to yourself, why would you reject your sexual desires? But if love is your highest purpose, then your desires must take second place. Otherwise, it is not biblical love.

COMPETING PERSPECTIVES ON MARRIAGE

The modern rift is not limited to sex. Marriage today looks dramatically different than it did a century ago. Throughout history, women bore the brunt of abusive behavior and bad marriages. Men held the right to divorce their wife, find a new one, and continue a career; but women often had no financial recourse if they chose to leave. For those who mustered up their courage, they often carried a stigma for the rest of their life.

Modern movements sought to even out the balance of power between men and women—for this we should be grateful and recognize there's still a lot of work to be done. However, the problem of sin has not been solved. Though women received an easier escape from an abusive marriage, good marriages still prove elusive in the modern equation.

Plenty of Humanists enjoy a life-long, healthy marriage, but the overall trend points a different direction. Half of first marriages now end in divorce; this is a five-fold increase from the last century. Marriage today is built on the Humanist premise of mutual benefit instead of the Kingdom foundation of sacrificial love. As a result, it is a partnership instead of a covenant.

Like all partnerships, this is based on both parties receiving a benefit. They each pursue their own self-interests, and believe they will thrive even more in doing so together. I'm not saying love is absent. I know many people genuinely love one another within this view of marriage, but the foundational premise looks different than the Kingdom's perspective.

Modern views of love might address some historic problems, but in doing so it misses God's ideal. It's built on preserving self, the very opposite of sacrifice. A Humanist might commit to a marriage and work through the difficulties, but it's hard to stick with it once the marriage becomes a hindrance to his or her dreams. For more than half of marriages in the United States, at some point the union is no longer mutually beneficial and thus the partnership is ended.

The Kingdom view of love will cost us everything. This love is seen in patiently caring for a spouse through the slow decline of Alzheimer's. This love is the choice to sacrifice a career so a spouse can pursue their calling. This love patiently endures their greatest weaknesses, their worst weeks, their biggest mistakes and still sticks with them, even at a cost to self.

This love is costly, but the price tag is worth it. Once you see the brush strokes of the Creator, His own life poured out on the canvas, the modern concept is exposed for the forgery it is.

GRACE TO RESTORE

Few people avoid the inevitable pain associated with sex and intimate relationships. Rather than revealing God's love, this may represent the greatest hurdle in a person's spiritual life. The sin of others, our own poor decisions, and the flawed expectations of culture hinder our ability to flourish.

Jesus modeled sacrificial love in His life on earth, but this alone proved insufficient. People saw His love from afar, but their sin still prevented them from living it. The world needed grace to love the way God intended. A diseased heart prevented each person from experiencing God's ideal. We all need a heart transplant.

Our selfishness hijacks our best intentions, hurting the people we love the most. Rather than receive a new heart, modern views of marriage instead provide a cynical look at human nature. It agrees that this love is impossible in our natural state, but rather than uphold the ideal, it instead restructures our relationships to function without it.

God offers a different path in the form of grace. We receive it from Jesus, not because we deserve it but instead because He loves us. He forgave our sin, which frees us to forgive the sin of others. No matter how broken our past, He works to restore and redeem what was lost.

His ideal is impossible, which is why Jesus died on a cross, rose again, and empowers us to live a new life by His Spirit. The love of God must first be received in order to be given away.

Grace doesn't necessarily mean we live free from the consequences of sin, whether ours or others. Not every marriage will make it. Occasionally one spouse is fully committed to sacrificial love yet still the other walks away. Abuse is still a major problem and is often based on manipulating love to maintain control. Enabling this sin is not love, and therefore boundaries are important. Occasionally, sin has so badly destroyed a relationship it cannot recover.

We will suffer the pain of sin in this life, but we live with hope. Jesus holds us in the darkest places. He restores us through the worst afflictions of this world. A relationship may never be fully mended. We may never truly atone for what we've done. But even in our deepest brokenness, Jesus will never forsake us. Our love may fail, but His will not. This revelation allows us to keep going, no matter what.

I understand how the pain of this life causes people to lose their ideals, but what a tragedy if we lose the ideal of sacrificial love. The love of Jesus carries us even when a spouse fails to meet our needs. He empowers us to love through the midst of our own pain. Don't settle for a forgery. Don't lose sight of the purity of Christ's love. Keep the ideal, though we fall short.

Sacrificial love is the key for Kingdom living, but even while we strive for it, remember that our feeble attempts pale in comparison to the One who loved us first. Fix your eyes on this, and you'll find power and grace for whatever this life may hold.

CHAPTER 8

SELF-ACTUALIZATION VS. SERVICE

Management fads drive me crazy. It's the leftover scars from my days in business school. Each trend started with an innovation that led to results within some company. A consultant discovered it, passed it off to researchers, and then eventually wrote a book. Before you know it, this latest buzzword takes over all organizations on earth. Apparently, everyone is looking for a silver bullet to cure their decades of dysfunction.

In my day, the word "synergy" was widely considered a magical solution for every problem. It seemed like merely whispering the term would solve the world's difficulties. I still don't know what "synergy" meant in practical terms, but it sure looked good on motivational posters.

My frustration with fads peaked while I was in college, particularly during the semester when all my courses conspired to teach the same theory of the psychologist Abraham Maslow. Yes, his theories influenced a lot of people, but I was a business major, not a philosopher. His concept of a "hierarchy of needs" described human motivation in profound ways, but I struggled to understand how it influences business accounting. Someone's good idea may not always be your solution. At some point, we need to determine whether the fad we follow leads us to the results we want.

Despite my frustrations with business school, Maslow's theory holds a lot of relevance for our worldview discussion. I'm thankful to know those hours of repetitive boredom weren't wasted. This teaching is influential and grew far beyond the scope of a typical fad; today, its influence reaches across society to such an extent I believe we've stopped questioning whether it is right. His viewpoint is deeply ingrained and affects just about everyone, even if you've never heard his name.

For the uninitiated, let me explain the idea. Maslow taught that a consistent set of needs motivates all humans. Some needs exist on a fundamental level and, until we meet these, we cannot progress to the next layer of development. The idea is often portrayed in the form of a hierarchal pyramid.

For example, the need for food and shelter is at the bottom, or most basic level, while the need for esteem is closer to the top. You need both, but until the need for sustenance is met, it's difficult to focus on anything else. Each person moves up the ladder of needs progressively, advancing from provision to safety to belonging to esteem, with each stage representing a higher plane of human fulfillment.

The top layer, however, is the pinnacle of human flourishing. To Maslow, this represented what he called "self-actualization." The term describes the process of identifying your true self—essentially the alignment of your passions, giftings, and dreams. We learn from his theory that there is more to life than steady employment or even a loving family. Each person holds a unique blueprint for personal fulfillment, and we all must learn to discover this map for ourselves. Until we do so, we'll never truly thrive.

I see Maslow's philosophy realized throughout our modern world, whether he is given credit or not. People routinely quit a lucrative job to pursue a more fulfilling occupation. At one level it's not rational, but when we recognize they're seeking to self-actualize, it all makes sense. Furthermore, their behavior is celebrated throughout our culture. We esteem the people willing to risk in order to break through into their highest place of fulfilment.

Personality quizzes have rapidly proliferated across the internet in recent years, largely because we all seek to better understand ourselves, presumably so we then might find our path to self-actualizing. This phenomenon is a recent development in human history. A massive effort to pursue self-expression and fulfillment dominates our culture. Most popular advice encourages us to take these steps. Don't get trapped doing something you don't love. Go chase your dream.

For some, this emphasis is overwhelming. Many people live immobilized by the countless opportunities. Perhaps the skyrocketing anxiety rates have something to do with *our* obsession with *our* ability to *self*-actualize to find *self*-fulfillment. We fear that in committing to one path we might miss another, which might even lead to greater flourishing. We live as products of an affluent age, freeing us to dream beyond living day-to-day to question life's purpose. Maslow's philosophy provides the goal for our pursuit, but is it leading to great fulfillment? I believe our self-centered obsession actually blocks us from the life we seek.

SELF-ACTUALIZATION AND THE KINGDOM

It's easy to see how this philosophy aligns with Humanism and thus fits within our culture. Maslow was considered a leading Humanist scholar in his generation. But this theory has also spread across Christendom and represents a worldview conflict, one which goes largely unrecognized.

The Kingdom and Humanist worldviews diverge in their approach to human nature, but Maslow's theory deeply influences both. Believers may intensely push back against the sexual ethics of Humanism, but the equally Humanistic concept of prioritizing self is given a free pass; in fact, it's often taught in churches.

Many Christian leaders teach a self-focused message, with some even explicitly calling us to put ourselves first. This is often a clumsy attempt to empower people with low self-esteem. A worthy cause but a dangerous approach that undercuts the Gospel message.

Most preach a subtler view; in fact, I doubt they're even aware of it. The problem is not necessarily the teaching points but rather the emphasis on self. We will never thrive if we're at the center of our lives. Only in embracing the death on the cross do we find resurrection life. Jesus provides our new identity, new purpose, and new strength to overcome whatever obstacle we face. When we take the attention off Him and put it onto ourselves, we miss out on the power of God in our lives.

The Christian variant of self-actualization focuses on spiritual gifts, individual calling, and dreams—all vaguely corresponding with God's dreams, or so we assume. We too strive to self-actualize, but we've dressed it up with spiritual terminology. The following sequence shapes our contemporary view of God: He is a kind father who wants us to thrive in this life; therefore, He must meet our various needs, which includes creating the environment for us to chase our passions. We assume this will occur relatively quickly because life is short, and it's cruel to make us suffer by not instantly providing for us, especially when He clearly has the power to do so.

It all neatly fits Maslow's Hierarchy of Needs and its Humanist foundations. If left unchecked, our demands soon overshadow our relationship with God. Any deficits prove a failure on His part. Many believers focus their spiritual attention on how God will meet his or her needs. Viewed through the lens of human interaction, it looks like a one-sided relationship. Furthermore, the role of God as the authority is subtly discarded, and He instead is demoted to a service-provider.

I've probably provoked a bit of outrage with the last few paragraphs. It's because I fear we've created an entitled view of God. Please don't blame a younger generation for this. Creeping Humanism is the cause, a decades-old trend which shows no sign of abating.

I see relatively little awareness or pushback against this modern tendency. We've welcomed the philosophy like a Trojan horse into the Church. It appears spiritual on the surface, masking the self-focused nature underneath a layer of Christian buzzwords.

Perhaps our modern viewpoint results from an overreaction to a past era which emphasized the authority of Christ to such an extent that the Church lost sight of His love. But now the pendulum has swung the opposite direction, and the problem is reversed. Neither represent the fullness of His character. Jesus serves us, but He is not our servant. He is Judge, He is King, and He is Lord. But equally, He is love, He is kind, and He is patient. We don't get to pick and choose which of these traits we want, while rejecting those we don't.

The root problem is self-centeredness. We want a relationship with God, but only on our terms. I wholeheartedly believe God wants us to thrive, will provide for us, and created us with unique gifts and passions. The truth of these statements isn't the issue. Our mistake occurs when we view these truths through the lens of a self-focused life. We reinterpret Him through our own desires.

Think of it in strictly human terms and consider a parent, close friend, or spouse who sacrificially loves you. They serve you because they genuinely want you to thrive. The relationship is a wonderful gift, but if you develop an entitled view of their love, you will destroy the intimacy. No one enjoys a relationship with someone who is self-centered and entitled. How many of us have done the same thing to God?

Hopefully this provokes some conviction—we all fall into this trap to some extent. Fortunately, God still loves us no matter how badly we've messed up. That's the power and beauty of His love, and it will never change. The question is how well we love Him in return.

A BIBLICAL PERSPECTIVE

Every generation tends to emphasize some Bible verses to the neglect of others. Psalm 37:4 is our culture's life verse, declaring the Lord will "give you the desires of your heart." I see it everywhere.

We interpret the famous passage through a Humanist lens and end up with a spiritual promise guaranteeing God will allow us to fully self-actualize in this life. We use the verse to sanctify our dreams and passions, reasoning that whatever we desire is something God put there and promises to give us.

The modern interpretation overlooks the first part of the verse, which instructs us first to, "Delight yourself in the LORD." The Psalmist called us to delight in the Lord, to let go of our cravings and worldly desires, and to live content in His presence. This is the key to understanding the passage.

He will give us the desires of our heart because our heart's desire is more of Him. This verse teaches the opposite of our popular interpretation. Yes, God absolutely intends for us to thrive in this life, but it will not be the path of Maslow. Us seeking to maximize ourselves is not the solution; instead, we flourish when we focus on Jesus above the things of this world, and even our own needs.

We'll never live satisfied when self reigns on the throne of our life. It's a paradox our culture cannot understand. Craig Gay calls it, "the despairing failure of the distinctively modern cult of self-fulfillment to satisfy the soul."[42] The path of Humanism teaches us to prioritize the things we feel lead to the greatest satisfaction. The Kingdom teaches us to die to ourselves and embrace a new life in Jesus.

Consider the following verses and contrast them to our modern culture:

"The heart is deceitful above all things and beyond cure. Who can understand it?" Jeremiah 17:9

"But seek first his kingdom and his righteousness, and all these things [worries of this world] will be given to you as well."
Matthew 6:33

"Whoever does not take up their cross and follow me is not worthy of me. Whoever finds their life will lose it, and whoever loses their life for my sake will find it." Matthew 10:38-39

"Whoever wants to be my disciple must deny themselves and take up their cross daily and follow me." Luke 9:23

"For we who are alive are always being given over to death for Jesus' sake, so that his life may also be revealed in our mortal body. So then, death is at work in us, but life is at work in you."
2 Corinthians 4:11-12

"Therefore we do not lose heart. Though outwardly we are wasting away, yet inwardly we are being renewed day by day. For our light and momentary troubles are achieving for us an eternal glory that far outweighs them all. So we fix our eyes not on what is seen, but on what is unseen, since what is seen is temporary, but what is unseen is eternal." 2 Corinthians 4:16-18

"I will boast all the more gladly about my weaknesses, so that Christ's power may rest on me. That is why, for Christ's sake, I delight in weaknesses, in insults, in hardships, in persecutions, in difficulties. For when I am weak, then I am strong."
2 Corinthians 12:9-10
"Do nothing out of selfish ambition or vain conceit. Rather, in humility value others above yourselves, not looking to your own interests but each of you to the interests of the others."
Philippians 2:3-4

"This is how we know what love is: Jesus Christ laid down his life for us. And we ought to lay down our lives for our brothers and sisters." 1 John 3:16

These passages reveal a vastly different roadmap to fullness compared to what our culture teaches; in fact, this shapes the whole narrative of Scripture. Reflect on the example of every single hero in the New Testament, and you'll discover they all share a common theme of learning to die to self and find life in God. Jesus modeled sacrificial love. He served His followers, He surrendered His rights, and He laid down His very life. His example became the standard for the early church. The life of a disciple proved costly for each one of the Twelve as they embraced His legacy.

Consider the life of Paul in light of our modern obsession with chasing our dreams and passions. The apostle studied under the famous Rabbi Gamaliel. He received the best training in Jewish law, especially compared to the rest of the church leaders who were uneducated fishermen. He passionately cared for the Jews; his letter to the Romans[43] described his deep anguish for his people. His dreams, giftings, and passions all aligned in reaching the Jews. Obviously, Paul should minister to the Jews living in Israel. Yet, of all the apostles, God chose Paul to preach to the Gentiles in Asia. How would you respond to Paul's calling? Many of us would angrily blame God for hijacking our dreams.

It gets worse. Paul never saw his calling fulfilled, at least this side of Heaven. I've often wondered if, at the end of his life, he even considered his work a success. As Paul marched to the executioner, internal disputes rocked the Church. Heresy grew rampant, legalistic teaching continued to spread, and various challenges arose against his authority—all increasing throughout his last years. The future seemed uncertain.

External factors also threatened the Church's survival. Paul died in the first major systemic persecution of believers,

and the might of Rome appeared poised to destroy the followers of Jesus. This instability also affected his nation and Israel
stood on the brink of civil war. The violent insurrection ultimately led to the complete destruction of Jerusalem. Paul went
to his death amidst gathering storm clouds, threatening everything he cared about most.

The luxury of time distorts our perspective. We recognize
his legacy. We know Paul's letters shaped the New Testament. We
see how the seeds of the Church continued to sprout across the
Empire, and in the coming centuries, spread across the entire
world. We can better assess his life's work. But what did he feel?

Through the eyes of a modern believer, Paul's life appears
cruel. God blocked him from his passions, and Paul never
saw the fulfillment of his dreams. I believe his later years held
significant pain and insecurity. Yet this man changed the world
like few ever have.

It's no accident that Paul's view of Heaven proved his
greatest revelation when you consider his life experience. Eternity's scoreboard is different than Maslow's. Striving to maximize yourself will lead you to a different place compared to a
life seeking to die to yourself. One is the Gospel; the other looks
suspiciously western.

The concept of dying to self, of choosing a path of sacrifice,
of considering others better than ourselves, and of laying down
our dreams for the sake of another is completely alien in our
culture. This prompts the question, does your life look more like
Paul or Maslow? Do your desires, dreams, and passions rule? Or
have you embraced the death and resurrection of the cross?

APPLYING THE PRINCIPLE

I see a lot of believers obsessing over "God's will for my life"
and spending significant energy determining their spiritual gifts.
Many take this knowledge and use it to seek to customize ministry
that fits them. We've learned to use spiritual terms, but the underlying motivation looks a lot like the world. While it's certainly

wisdom to seek "God's will," I think many of us live much more concerned about "my life." The questions aren't the problem. In fact, they can be quite helpful. The issue is when they become a tool for self-centered living dressed up in spiritual terms.

Instead, we should first learn "God's will." Not many people start by seeking to serve the greatest needs. We look inward before looking outward. Our service is often tinged with selfishness. We want to serve, but only within our giftings, passions, and convenience.

Most people remain unaware of their conflicted motivations; we're simply reflecting our culture. I do it, and I bet you do as well. My point is not to condemn anyone. I believe most believers genuinely do want to serve, but I wonder if we forgot what it looks like.

Imagine a completely different approach. Before spending time analyzing your strengths, start by inquiring about the needs of others. Ask what ministry within your church needs help. Look into service opportunities in your community. Don't worry too much about where you fit and instead focus on helping others.

What if God intended your greatest legacy to take place outside of your giftings? It seems almost heretical to consider, but remember, He's the one who said it's in our weakness we're made strong.

This doesn't mean we lose sight of our individuality; instead, it's a call to change our focus. When you seek to serve more than to meet your own needs, then all those personality profiles and gifts assessments can prove quite helpful.

Furthermore, I do believe it's important to take care of yourself. You hold intrinsic worth and are deeply loved by God; He will often lead you into times of rest. Your human relationships should be reciprocal. If you're doing all the serving while others do nothing, you may be enabling an unhealthy environment. Set boundaries and don't feel guilty for taking time for self-care. But in doing so, avoid the Humanist message that life is all about you.

Self-awareness is important in our quest to serve others. Our maturity is largely based on a better understanding of ourselves, including our gifts and weaknesses. Over time you learn to generally turn down opportunities that rest outside of your strength. This is healthy because you know the specific places you can best contribute to the needs of others. The crux of the issue rests in your *motivations*—do you seek a role to self-actualize or to serve?

This question has affected every one of my career steps. It started when I was between jobs in college. I wanted to use my time wisely, so I initiated with my church to volunteer ten hours weekly until I found employment elsewhere. It soon turned into a part-time job offer as an administrative assistant. I wasn't particularly qualified, but it was the greatest need and a whole lot better than my previous jobs.

The work proved a steep learning curve and forced me to rapidly develop my skillset. This led to increased ministry opportunities, and eventually grew into a full-time pastoral position with a college ministry. Each step built on the last and each focused on the need of the ministry. I didn't have a particular plan. Many years later, and with many steps in between, my current role now fits how God wired me. I feel like the luckiest guy on earth. But I didn't start in my dream job. Instead, it all developed over time, as I sought to meet the needs of those around me.

A service approach won't always lead to tangible results. I once taught myself to play guitar to lead small group worship. Those few weeks weren't particularly worshipful for anyone. I soon realized the best way to serve the group was to stop. My greatest contribution was to quickly motivate a more gifted individual to step up because he couldn't take it anymore.

I've held a wide range of ministry roles over the years. In each new opportunity, I fight to stop focusing on self-actualizing. This requires a lot of effort because a self-focus is still so deeply ingrained in me. I'm not always successful. My frustration levels are a good indicator of my motivations. The source of my angst is often some blocked goal of mine. Rather than stew in self-pity, if I take time to re-center on Jesus, I always find fresh perspective.

The irony of it all is that the more I die to self, the more I find life. This is how the Kingdom works, and our world does not understand it. An others-first approach will eventually put you into the place of your greatest gifting. God advocates for you when you advocate for others. The reason God gave you gifts is to serve others, not to feel good about yourself.

The best way to serve is normally within the context of your giftings. I realize this is nuanced. I led worship in my small group because I sought to serve, but people were not helped by my attempt because I wasn't gifted. I do not regret the decision, but at the same time, I also stepped out of the role when I realized it was not a good fit. It's far better to fail attempting to help people than it is to live paralyzed by all the options our culture presents or, worse, by demanding people create special roles just for us.

This same approach allowed me to discover giftings I never dreamed of. I never aspired to write. It was only when the ministry needed to rewrite a manual that I attempted it. Eventually, this first step led to another, with an opportunity to serve someone else by editing their book. Only much later did I find the opportunity to write my own.

Our motivations are the primary issue. I do believe it's important to discover our strengths and develop an accurate assessment of our abilities, but this is just a tool, not a goal. Learn how God wired you so you can determine how to serve your family, your church, and your community.

While you develop the strengths God gave you, remember that sometimes the best way to serve others rests outside of your giftings. Ultimately, I believe you'll best serve others in the context of your gifts, but this will not always be true. A good litmus test to determine whether we're motivated by Maslow or Jesus is to ask whether you'd do something outside of your strengths if that's the best way to serve others.

Our deepest needs will never be met by finding our identity in our giftings. We will not be truly satisfied with the perfect job. God created us for more. It's only when we discover our life in Him that we learn to live our life on earth. Jesus described this process as being "born again." We died to our old way of living and its attempts to find self-worth, and now live a new life. If our motivations look like the world's, then something is wrong.

Most people will never hold a ministry job. The principle may seem obvious at church, but unrealistic at work. In a business environment, you will need to assert yourself and negotiate for promotions. You will need to decline opportunities or move on to a new company for a better position. These actions are not inherently wrong. It's all about motivation. What's the point of your career? Are you driven by the need for more money or influence? If so, you'll never be satisfied.

I know many people who've turned down a prestigious position because of its impact on their children and their ability to serve in the church. I know others who hold influential jobs but work hard to keep their motivations pure and view their workplace as a mission field. Both hold the right perspective.

Life is complicated. I cannot advise each person's unique scenario, but I challenge you to focus on your internal motivation. What's driving you?

Your self-worth is not based on your spiritual gifts. Your identity does not depend upon your talents. God adopted you as His child, which makes you royalty. He placed His Spirit inside of you to empower you. He validated you before all Heaven and earth. You don't need some special ability to be someone special. You already are significant, so take your abilities and go serve someone else.

CHAPTER 9

THE IMPORTANCE OF THE CHURCH

We live in the age of individualized faith. I increasingly hear things like, "For me, going to church is watching a sunset" from Christians who choose to step away from organized faith. Most of them still hold devout beliefs and love Jesus. The pain of church life caused their departure, not their doctrine, so they chose to leave church entirely to rediscover their spiritual life outside of any formal structure with other people.

This trend results from people burning out and, in the aftermath, choosing to focus on a simpler faith. While every situation is different, each person establishes a new, distinct foundation for his or her walk with God. I agree that we don't need a worship band, hymns, professional sermons, or a building to worship God. I see how, if we aren't careful, modern liturgies can distract us in our pursuit of God instead of facilitating genuine spiritual growth.

I can agree with many of these statements, but worry about the larger trend. We've deconstructed church, talking about all the things *it is not*, to such an extent that I fear we've lost sight of the beauty of *what it is*, and *what it can be*. The result is the belief that walking on the beach and enjoying a sunset is now church—simple and pure, a personalized place to meet with God.

I understand the struggle, but I passionately believe quitting the local church is the wrong approach. It may temporarily ease the pain native to community life; however, this "liberty" will come at a great cost. Choosing to separate from the church will eventually carry us into the waiting arms of our society's worldview, and it will rob us of the chance to model a Kingdom culture to the world.

We may need to reform the church, or even reinvent it, but we cannot abandon it, no matter how appealing the option appears. I believe our ability to thrive amid a worldview clash is directly dependent on the strength of our churches. We have work to do. Let's start by looking at the challenges.

THE CHALLENGES OF CHURCH

Two primary factors cause people to leave. Negative events are the obvious cause. People depart due to a pastor's sexual or financial impropriety, hypocrisy, a power struggle amongst the leadership, a church split, and unresolved conflict, to name a few.

These stories grab the spotlight, but most people don't leave after just one bad experience. A recent study revealed people joined an average of four different churches before making the decision to leave church altogether. Most never intended to leave and only quit after experiencing the same problems in multiple places.

The growing desire for individualization is the second factor influencing those departing. Individualism teaches that one-size-fits-all solutions don't work. Each person demands customized solutions for just about everything in our modern world, including our faith. But we soon discover the difficulty of finding any organization which perfectly aligns with us, so we mix and match to find our perfect fit.

Society has progressed from the age of Walmart to the age of Amazon. The first offered a big box solution for just about any problem. We just showed up and found our aisle. The second offers customized solutions from our living room, giving us the freedom to meet our needs without the hassle of the crowds. Church trends look similar.

Why go to the trouble of getting the family out the door, dealing with people problems, and wading through inefficient systems when you can find a more spiritual experience watching a sunset by yourself? Besides, if you need a sermon, the world's best preachers are just a click away, and Google reviews will ensure you aren't confronted with something that makes you uncomfortable. Customize to your heart's content while avoiding the challenges of commitment.

Combine the two factors—the pain of church life and our desire for individualization—and this trend makes a lot of sense. I doubt it will slow down anytime soon.

I relate to those who walk away. I've felt burdened by ministry responsibilities. I've woken up many Sunday mornings wishing I could be somewhere else. I've been bored in sermons. I've watched friends leave. I've felt the pain of a declining church as the room shrank each week until it felt like a shell of the past. I've felt the pain of a growing church, waking up to realize the intimacy of our tight-knit group was lost forever. I've lived on the edge of burnout after serving in the same role for well over a decade. I've disagreed with decisions. I've felt loss with changes.

However much I empathize with the pain inherent in church, I'm deeply concerned with the mindset. Church is not your spiritual gas station. God designed His Church to meet some of our needs, but that is not its main purpose. We've substituted the mission of the Church for one of its benefits.

I believe Humanism has bled into our perspective on the Body of Christ, and I worry this will undercut the most effective

129

way for us to create a lasting Kingdom culture. Our consumerism causes us to view organizations, including church, according to what we get from them and how they bring us fulfillment. Amazon meets our shopping needs. Craft coffee keeps us awake. Church inspires us spiritually. Everything has a role to contribute to our well-rounded, thriving life. Except that's not the Kingdom worldview.

Jesus modeled a starkly different mindset. The final gathering of His disciples prior to His execution proved a seminal moment in the life of the Church. Much of John's gospel took place around this dinner table, later known as The Last Supper. He used this moment to teach the power of serving and install it as a central value for His disciples. We need to approach church life the way of Jesus, not the way of our culture.

For most of history, people shared the road with animals and all their droppings, few roads were ever paved, and the result was one giant mess. Many cultures still consider the soles of the feet a dirty part of the body from this legacy. Rich households employed servants to clean the feet of guests to keep the nastiness outside, and, understandably, this was not a desirable job.

At the beginning of dinner, Jesus removed His outer cloak, dropped to a knee, and washed His disciples' feet. His hands cleansed the filth of the world, and He took on the role of the lowliest servant. His actions shocked His followers. I worry that we no longer recognize the power of Jesus' radical act. Will we take on the same posture toward the people of God? Will we do the dirty, difficult, and thankless work? Or do we approach the meal demanding our needs be met and our feet get cleaned?

Jesus' example provided a powerful statement to His followers. His ministry occurred in the aftermath of King Herod's reign, a tyrant famous for his lavish building projects while the country suffered under financial burdens. Jesus demonstrated a drastically different approach to leadership, one built on sacrificially loving others. He then charged us to do the same. It was countercultural to His first disciples in the same way it is for us today.

Don't give up on the church. It's hard to wash someone's feet when you're by yourself watching a sunset. The Church of Jesus was never meant to be a service provider for our spiritual life; instead, it's the place we serve others. It will get messy because people are a mess, including you and me.

Jesus suffered at the hands of His Church. One member betrayed Him and contributed to His death. His closest friends fell asleep when He needed comfort the most. Everyone deserted Him when the trouble came. Jesus was no stranger to church pain, but He still called us His Body and His Bride.

The church provides wonderful benefits, a community to belong, a place to contribute, and deep spiritual experiences, but we've missed the point when our needs become our primary motivation. Sacrificial love calls us to serve others. It's when we lay down our life that we find it. We will remain dissatisfied whenever our desires serve as our primary motivation. This is the paradox of the Kingdom.

A commitment to the Church does not require you to stay in a dysfunctional fellowship. Work it out as best you can, but at times people need to leave. God also might call you to a new place of service even when everything is going well. We may move around individual local churches for legitimate reasons, but we need to reject the unhealthy pull of our culture which seeks to isolate us by leaving the church altogether.

It's important to recognize that a healthy church might take on a non-traditional structure. The specific ways a church is organized—buildings, service style, and organization—are generally neutral. Some models might contribute more to health than others, but people are the main problem. God often calls people to innovate new ways to express His Body. This is healthy. Quitting His Body entirely is not.

THE CHURCH CREATES CULTURE

Humanity is inherently social. We find our identity through our interactions with people. Success, failure, even rebellion, can only be discovered through its connection to the same in others. Everyone is influenced by others. We call this culture. Whether it's our family, friends, city, or church, our sense of self is not formed in isolation. The culture we adhere to will shape us. I believe this is a theme throughout the New Testament.

To live a Kingdom culture, we first must discover our identity in Jesus and determine success by His Word, not our cultural standing. But no matter the strength of our spiritual life, we are still fundamentally social. This was not an accident. It was hardwired into us at creation and declared "good" by the Creator.

Sin distorts the power of culture. What God intends to propel us in our faith often becomes the thing which pulls us away. Despite the challenges, God never abandoned His design, instead He redeemed it. The result is His Church. The Church is meant to fully express the Kingdom culture.

The Church is global and comprises all believers, but it's also local—a community of people who commit to one another and to the ways of God. These people live differently than the world around them. Their relationships provide a place of strength to resist the pull of the world, and it also shines as a beacon of life to those trapped in darkness. That's the plan at least; reality is often different.

The Church is flawed, and often surgery is needed to maintain a healthy Body. However, too many people view euthanasia as the only solution for the pain. Watching a sunset will not create a Kingdom culture, no matter how worshipful. You need a personal life in God, and you also need a place to commit to other believers. Go spend time in nature to meet with Jesus, and then go serve a local church.

Stepping away from the Body doesn't immunize you from the power of culture; instead, it just changes which one will shape you. As Humanism expands throughout our society, the Church will need to grow stronger to thrive. Isolation virtually guarantees we will succumb to the world.

God shaped my life through a variety of spiritual experiences. Some of these moments occurred in stillness, while others took place in a corporate service. But no matter how dynamic, no one event changed my life. God transformed my life through community. More importantly, God empowered me to remain transformed through community. I'm not strong enough to swim against the current of our culture alone, and neither are you. God designed us to need each other.

GOD'S INTENTION FOR THE CHURCH

Part of the problem is our lack of clarity regarding the purpose of the Church. There is no New Testament equivalent to the book of Leviticus. The Old Testament book prescribed the structure of Jewish worship in detail, down to the clothing the priests wore during a religious service.

I find it remarkable that there is not a single book in the New Testament commanding the order of worship and the organization of the Church. The Book of Acts is a historical account of the Church, and provides some clues, but it's not descriptive enough to be definitive.

One simple book could have settled for all eternity the exact job description of a lead pastor, the right way to preach, the color of the carpet in the sanctuary, and the proper size of a congregation. In the Old Testament, nothing was left to chance. The entire religious structure was provided, so why is it missing for us?

I believe the answer is found in what we were given, which is our new identity in Christ and a charge to live accordingly. We died to the culture of the world and are reborn into the culture of Heaven. Learning to live this culture is far more important than the systems regarding how we do it. If we get the culture of the church right, we'll naturally develop the right structure. But no amount of systems can save a broken culture.

Leaving the church is the wrong approach. A system may be broken, but abandoning the model entirely will not fix the problem. The main problem is within each one of us, and until we commit to live a Kingdom culture, we cannot outrun the pain unless we isolate ourselves. Too many Christians spend time arguing about the details of how a church runs rather than letting God transform them—their character, their worldview, and their view of others. This is a primary cause for the pain that forces so many to leave. Get the culture right and there's grace for everything else.

The reason for this oversight is quite simple: It's much easier to develop a structure than it is to develop a culture. Systems can be measured, and good systems often lead to increased growth. Systems can be mass-produced and taught in a classroom setting. By contrast, culture is ambiguous, difficult to track, and hard to build. Church growth places tremendous pressure on structures. Most pastors do care about culture but feel like their life is spent playing catch up.

To thrive in an opposing worldview, we must resolve to live a Kingdom culture together in committed relationships, no matter the cost. It's not convenient, and sacrificial love is the opposite of consumerism. My personal time with God may be spent watching a sunset, but my church must be washing the feet of broken people.

If this sounds extreme, consider the ministry of Jesus. He spent three whole years modeling culture for just twelve men. Of all the options for the Messiah to spend His time, He chose to disciple a few misfits into a Kingdom culture. That also sounds extreme. Do you see the church through His eyes? Or through the lens of Humanism?

Culture cannot be mass-produced, but if the culture is healthy, it will be massively reproduced. People long to experience authentic Kingdom community. Too few examples exist within our churches, especially compared to the many negative examples. But God empowered you as a solution, so go do something about it.

A CITY ON THE HILL

The Church is the agent God uses to establish His Kingdom on earth, whether we like it or not. We're the pillar and support of the truth. We're the manifold wisdom of God. We're the Body of Christ, His literal hands and feet on this earth. We're His Bride.

It's sobering to consider the significance of our role. Jesus inaugurated a Kingdom and set out on a mission, but He did not complete it. Instead, He ascended into Heaven, empowered us by His Spirit, and left behind His Body to finish the job. We hold the answer the world so desperately needs. There is no Plan B.

Modern worldviews cannot lead humanity into the light. Racism, oppressive governments, and systemic injustice contribute to the darkness, but people are the source. Until we fix us, we cannot walk free. Jesus provided the solution in His own blood and commanded His Church to be the light for those still trapped in darkness.

The Book of Matthew contains the longest recorded sermon of Jesus. Stretching over three chapters, the Sermon on the Mount provides a glimpse into the new Kingdom culture. His teaching revolutionized the disciples' view of prayer, giving, righteousness, mercy, and success. Some Bible scholars refer to the message as the "Upside-Down Kingdom," because it so thoroughly contrasts with the ways of the world.

New worldviews come and go throughout history, each attempting to lead humanity out of the darkness, but they inevitably fail because they depend on the strength of people. A few generations will buy into the view for a while, until it runs its course and is replaced by a new, equally ineffective mindset. Jesus upended our view of everything because only His way of living will set us free.

In the middle of describing the Kingdom, Jesus paused to speak a word of identity over His people, stating, "You are the light of the world. A town built on a hill cannot be hidden." These short sentences hold profound implications for us, both as individuals and as the Church. It ties into the theme of light and darkness which runs throughout the Scriptures, from the very beginning to the end.

In the first three verses of Genesis, we find the universe in total darkness. Darkness today is vaguely uncomfortable, a forgotten dread whose fullness we seldom feel. This was not always the case. There was no substance to the ever-present blackness before time. It reigned absolute, its identity wholly defined as the absence of light.

Into this void of nothing God spoke, His breath radiating into the world as light. Light is the seed of creation, something into the nothing. Light brings beauty, light provides perspective, and without it, life is impossible. Light originated in God and cannot exist apart from Him.

Sin plunged man back into the emptiness, cutting us off from the Source. Sin's penalty is death and darkness. We now live in the fading glow of creation, alive for a moment but doomed to navigate spiritual darkness. We exist as a mere shadow of what was, a faint memory of what could have been.

In the first four verses of John, we find the universe in darkness once again. There was no real substance in the ever-present spiritual blackness. Sin reigned absolute, our identity forever lost in the absence of God's light.

Into this void of nothing God spoke. This time His Word entered the world as a man. Jesus is the Seed of the new creation. Instead of sin's darkness, He is the light of the world.[45] Rather than sin's curse of death, His light is the life of men.

Consider the profound implications of Jesus' declaration that we are the light of the world. If Jesus had not spoken it, we'd consider His words heresy. We introduced the darkness into God's creation. How can we be the light?

Jesus lived as a light source in a dark world. When we received new life in Him, we also received His Spirit within us, and we too transformed into a light source. Darkness has no power over the light. Darkness only exists in light's absence; they are not equals. The only way to stop a light is to cover it up or turn it out. Every believer is called a light. Reflect on the power of this statement—this is your destiny. Fight to keep your light ablaze.

Our personal calling is important, but the next sentence is even more significant. Though our individual call to shine is powerful, when we come together, an incredible thing happens and we see "a town built on a hill that cannot be hidden." One candle pierces the darkness, but a city of candles transforms it.

Have you ever gazed out an airplane window into the blackness of night, only to see the faint glow of a city on the horizon? With each passing minute, the entire landscape slowly changes, and a brilliant network of lights transforms the ground below. It's a breathtaking experience; I travel often but still pause to enjoy the wonder.

The light of a city is a beacon within the darkness. Individual candles may get snuffed out, but not a city ablaze. God intended His Church to shine like this type of a light. It happens when each of us first tends to our own wick by pursuing a vibrant life in God, and then choose to come together as His Church to model a new culture, a new worldview in the midst of the world around us.

One candle will not transform the atmosphere by itself. You might shine for a while, but without others to reignite you and tend your flame, your light will prove fleeting. Isolation robs us of our destiny.

Church life is painful. Watching a sunset is more enjoyable and personally fulfilling, but the Kingdom is bigger than our needs. We carry the light of Christ within us. The pull toward Humanism is strong, and its strength is building. On the one hand, I'm not worried. It will go the road of every other flawed worldview. But I am concerned for the countless multitudes who blindly follow its path.

What a tragedy if we isolate ourselves from the Body at the very hour in which we need to shine the most. It's a difficult task. We need to confront our own selfishness while also grappling with the sin of others, but we're not alone. I believe in the power and presence of God to lead us if we'll recommit to the local church.

Don't let your past define your view of the church. Get a fresh perspective, a biblical vision for what the church can be. Imagine a group of people who each seek God as their first priority, who love one another deeply, and who commit to sacrificially serve the needs of their community.

Imagine a church leading the way in maintaining financial integrity, in establishing authentic servant leadership, in welcoming the marginalized, in modeling reconciliation amongst racial groups, in repenting for its past, and in proclaiming hope for the future.

However far this seems from your experience, this is the Church established by Jesus. It's just a taste of the Kingdom culture He inaugurated. We need to stand on the Word of God. We need to contend for our inheritance. We may never see its fullness in this life, but I'd rather die trying than give up and accept the brokenness of the culture around me.

Don't lose your hope. Don't forsake meeting together. You need the church and the church needs you. I'm convinced that if we rediscover our calling and recommit to the local church, however it may look, Jesus will rebuild us into a city shining on a hill.

CHAPTER 10

THE GREATEST INJUSTICE

It was a humid spring day in the nation's capital. A faint chant echoed in the distance as I strolled across the National Mall. I passively listened to the protest but never quite understood the purpose. Instead, the echoing sound and chaotic streets jumbled together into an ambient noise, a fitting soundtrack for my afternoon in Washington, DC.

As I walked by, I wondered how often this scene repeats itself. Substitute in a different cause, hordes of tourists walking by, the traffic crawling past in an unending line–different lyrics, but the same song. A protest is the new normal, the soundtrack of a generation.

Our nation is awakening to countless example of injustice in our society. We've started to recognize how the undercurrents of misogyny, systemic racism, economic inequality, unconscious bias, and xenophobia create an unfair system of winners and losers, often based on nothing more than skin color or geography. Increasing numbers of people consider it a moral responsibility to respond in some way, such as protests in the Capitol, donations to nonprofits, volunteerism, and online activism.

It's an exciting time to be alive, especially for the marginalized. As a Christian, I'm grateful for the emphasis on justice. Jesus modeled a life of activism. He routinely cared for those who suffered at the hands of a majority culture. He noticed the people living on society's edge. He shone a light on hypocrisy. He reached across dividing lines of race and culture to love His neighbor. I may not always agree on each particular justice issue in culture, but I'm thankful people care.

For all the challenges in our nation's move into Humanism, the area of justice is a place of opportunity. It's a place of partnership between churches and their community. It's also a healthy point of accountability for the people of God. We live in a society focused on justice, while we preach a message of service. The world will prove quick to point out any discrepancies. It may get annoying, but it will also help us stay on track with what we claim to live.

THE GREATEST INJUSTICE

In our quest to root our systemic problems in society, we risk overlooking the greatest injustice of all: Nearly half of the world's population will live and die without a realistic chance of ever hearing the Gospel message. If you scoffed at my last sentence, it's probably because your view of justice is largely shaped by Humanism.

Humanists and believers may agree on a lot of social issues, but when it comes to the Great Commission, we hold opposing viewpoints. If you live with a Kingdom worldview, then there is no greater injustice on the planet than the reality of so many people remaining cut off from Christ. By contrast, a Humanist doesn't care at all, in fact, they may see it positively.

The difference is Humanism's view religion as an optional feature of life. To Humanists, there is no reason to impose a foreign view on people who find fulfillment in their traditional beliefs; in fact, new beliefs may lead to unnecessary pain and confusion. They believe we're all on the same path toward meaning and consider our exclusive statements about Jesus to be arrogant. A Humanist morality would challenge us to refocus our efforts on solving systemic problems in society and "finally do something positive in the world."

A true Kingdom worldview is radically different than Humanism, and for believers, there is no greater concern than the Gospel. You cannot hold both perspectives. If we allow Humanism to shape our view of justice, we may solve some of the world's problems but will overlook the worst injustice of all.

The broad agreement on other social areas hides this massive discrepancy. The Kingdom and Humanist moral codes agree on many other justice outcomes, but we need to remember there is a vast difference in the worldview. Even if we arrive at the same destination on a justice issue, we traveled a different path to get there.

The Gospel message permeates the Kingdom worldview in every way. It teaches that our sin holds us back from God and sabotages our potential. We cannot fix our sin in our own strength, and our only hope is a Savior. Jesus died to pay the penalty for our sin, and then rose again to conquer its power. He put His Spirit within us. His Spirit then transforms us from the inside out and allows us to sacrificially love others and overcome temptation. We access this salvation through faith in Jesus alone, which comes through hearing the message. If we accept this gift and surrender our lives to God, He restores us to a relationship with Him, both in this life and for all eternity. If not, we remain cut off from His grace now and forever.

Do you believe this? Because if you do, what injustice is greater than the reality of such a staggering number of people who will never hear this message? I wonder how many Christians have affirmed this *theologically* without ever embracing it *emotionally*. If we fail to recognize the Gospel for the cure it is, then we will not understand the justice imperative of the Great Commission.

Consider my statement with the following illustration: Imagine a pharmaceutical company developing a safe and cheap cure for cancer. Eight million people die annually from this type of disease, and tens of millions more suffer from it. Suddenly, with this new treatment, every life could be saved and each person spared the pain of the symptoms.

I believe most people agree on the incredible moral obligation to spread this treatment as rapidly as possible. Imagine the outcry if the company refused to produce the quantities needed to treat everyone or failed to distribute the cure to certain countries. In effect, they'd be signing death sentences for the sake of convenience and profit. If it every happens, I'll join you in the picket line.

Regardless of your worldview, you probably recognize this scenario represents a horrific injustice. Disease eradication is an important justice initiative. Often, whether you live or die is determined by where you live. What a tragedy. What an injustice.

Nonprofits work tirelessly to distribute vaccines and treatments to stop the spread of curable diseases around the world. Their efforts have seen great success, including the successful eradication of smallpox. These efforts disrupt local communities occasionally, but the countless lives saved overshadows any concerns.

Because we understand the destruction of disease, we also understand the power of a cure. This frames our perspective on eradication efforts. We cannot sit idly knowing people are dying from preventable illnesses. This is not an issue of cultural preference, as though some cultures prefer cancer or polio. I believe every person should have access to life-saving care, and we should work to make it happen. The cause is worth the sacrifice.

Do we take the same approach with the Gospel? We claim to hold the cure for sin, the root of all destruction on the planet, and we believe our message leads to eternal life. If we truly believe the Gospel message, we recognize the importance of distributing it to every person on the planet. Why aren't we more concerned about the injustice of its limited spread?

I once heard a missionary share the story of leading a person to the Lord in a tribe that was previously unreached with the message of Jesus. After surrendering to Jesus, the new believer asked, "How long has your tribe carried this hope?" The American answered that it had been many hundreds of years. The man held back tears and incredulously declared, "You've known this for centuries and yet only now come to tell us? Generations of my family have lived and died without ever knowing." The missionary listened and found no fitting words to respond to such a terrible injustice.

The sobering moment underscored the reality of what we preach. Do we believe Jesus is the only way to salvation? Do we believe He alone conquered sin? If so, we need to allow our faith to shape our worldview and, with it, our emotions. Too many of us live the other way around. We empathize with the emotions of our culture and allow it to shape our beliefs. I've even felt guilty for the emphasis we put on the Gospel. It's a sign of how deeply Humanism has affected my worldview.

A believer sees the Gospel as the cure for the world's worst problem. A Humanist sees it as a spiritual option for some people. To us, it's the most essential human right. To the other, it's an amenity that might help.

Because we view it through such a difference lens, we will arrive at completely different perspectives on the importance of proclaiming it. A Humanist will accuse us of forcing our beliefs on someone when they really need us to provide practical care. They see our missions efforts as a mismanagement of resources and potential hindrance to lasting transformation. By contrast, Christians see the Gospel as the most powerful change agent on earth.

Which view affects you most? Have you allowed Humanism to cloud your perspective? Do you feel guilty for proclaiming the exclusivity of Jesus? Do you seek to downplay your beliefs and purely focus on social efforts instead?

I believe the Gospel is more important than a cure for cancer. I believe it alone holds hope for humanity. I also believe God called His Church to proclaim this message to every person on this planet so that each person might have the chance to receive Christ's gift. I hold this view unapologetically.

THE POWER OF THE GOSPEL

The Gospel message alone provides hope for humanity because it deals with the root cause of our problems. Jesus removed our heart of sin and replaced it with His heart, sparking a complete transformation and radiating out into every aspect of our life. The power of God within us provides the strength to overcome all sorts of destructive behavior.

Sin is the root sickness of mankind and its symptoms touch every aspect of life. Injustice originated in sin. We may resolve one long-standing social problem through an awareness campaign, but the sinful heart remains intact apart from the Gospel.

The message of Jesus leads to eternal life, and it also leads to a renewed life on earth. By embracing the cross and the Resurrection, both individuals and ethnic groups will find power to overcome societal sin.

Through the teaching of Jesus, we see the intrinsic value and dignity of each person. Upon this foundation, we fight against racism, misogynism, and other forms of discrimination. Injustice is particularly difficult to combat because often the worst offenders were, at one time, the worst affected by someone else's sin, which then causes a cycle of destruction. The Gospel provides hope. Grace forgives our past, heals our pain, and teaches us to forgive. Without these, I don't believe a lasting transformation is possible. When retribution is the only solution for justice, we simply extend the problem.

Our salvation in Jesus leads us into a new way of living. The Gospel provides forgiveness for the past and also empowers us to live differently. The Holy Spirit convicts us of our sin, both individually and culturally, and then transforms us to embrace a new lifestyle. Our faith leads us to grow in Christ-like behavior by embracing a call to love, patience, kindness, goodness, self-control, and more. With this foundation we can overcome any problem in society.

Imagine a world built on sacrificial love, the fruit of the Spirit, forgiveness, and an authentic concern for our neighbor. Whatever the problem, these ingredients will lead to a lasting solution. But apart from this, we'll stay focused on managing symptoms without ever dealing with the root disease.

This theology does not provide an excuse for inaction on social issues. It's a false dichotomy that tries to force us to choose between the two. Christians should lead Gospel-centered lives and be deeply passionate about the needs of their community. In fact, to embrace the Kingdom requires you to care for others. The two are inseparable.

Let's preach Jesus while also educating the church on the impact of unconscious bias. Let's grow as disciples by engaging with the social needs in our community. Go volunteer in a lower-income public school. Start a friendship with someone from a different ethnic background. Work to fight injustice in your community. And, while doing so, find ways to support the Great Commission with your time, money, and prayer. The Kingdom is all of it.

The legacy of Cultural Christianity confuses the issue. Many Christians in eras past professed right doctrine and maintained appearances, but never allowed the Gospel to transform their life or their culture. Some believers even proclaimed that the primacy of the Gospel allowed them to ignore the needs in their community.

I believe many modern, secular viewpoints blatantly and unfairly overlook the incredible contributions of the Church in fighting global injustice. Christians do, and always have, led the way at every level of society. But we also need to confront places we tolerated injustice or disengaged from our communities, and instead focused on the four walls of our comfortable congregation.

We need to repent for a flawed past, but this is no excuse to abandon the Gospel. Christians have consistently led the world in social reform while proclaiming the saving grace of Jesus. The sin of some does not invalidate the message of hope. Let's lead the way in both spreading the Gospel while also engaging the practical needs of those around us. This is not an optional aspect of our faith; it is the very command of Jesus to His Church.

THE PRIMACY OF THE GREAT COMMISSION

The Kingdom starts with the Gospel and extends to transform every part of our world, including each place of systemic injustice. This is the mission of Jesus. He established a new Kingdom based on the love of God while overthrowing the systems of man. He conquered sin and empowered His people.

The problem is that He did not finish the job. Jesus left that to us. He inaugurated His Kingdom and empowered His people to complete the mission. There is no ambiguity in His commands to the Church.

Therefore go and make disciples of all nations, baptizing them in the name of the Father and of the Son and of the Holy Spirit, and teaching them to obey everything I have commanded you. And surely I am with you always, to the very end of the age. Matthew 28:19-20

He said to them, "Go into all the world and preach the gospel to all creation. Whoever believes and is baptized will be saved, but whoever does not believe will be condemned." Mark 16:15-16

*He told them, "This is what is written: The Messiah will suffer and rise from the dead on the third day, and repentance for the forgiveness of sins will be preached in his name to all nations, beginning at Jerusalem. You are witnesses of these things. I am going to send you what my Father has promised; but stay in the city until you have been clothed with power from on high."
Luke 24:46-49*

But you will receive power when the Holy Spirit comes on you; and you will be my witnesses in Jerusalem, and in all Judea and Samaria, and to the ends of the earth. Acts 1:8

All this is from God, who reconciled us to himself through Christ and gave us the ministry of reconciliation: that God was reconciling the world to himself in Christ, not counting people's sins against them. And he has committed to us the message of reconciliation. We are therefore Christ's ambassadors, as though God were making his appeal through us. We implore you on Christ's behalf: Be reconciled to God. 2 Corinthians 5:18-20

The Bible clearly commands the Church to live on mission, and this was reflected in the lifestyle of the early believers. The Book of Acts is the story of the first generation of believers and their quest to proclaim this message. The whole book is a narrative of mission. Paul's letters were all written in the context of his missionary journeys. God's mission shapes the whole New Testament.

A few generations after the Resurrection, Christians spread to the furthest limits of the Roman Empire in the west and far into Asia in the east—all without the benefit of modern technology. They earnestly embraced the Great Commission at great cost to themselves. We're here today as a result.

Whatever problems we see in our world, it's worth recognizing how far we've come since the Gospel first took root. Most modern social justice originated in the Church. The sacrifice of long-forgotten believers injected the mercy of God into our society. Someone sacrificed so that we might thrive.

Now it's our turn. Thousands of entire ethnic groups remain unreached with the message of Jesus. Countless individuals, including our neighbors and co-workers, have never heard a clear Gospel presentation. This is an injustice, and Jesus appointed us as His ambassadors to fix it.

CONFLICTING EMOTIONS

From a biblical perspective, this may seem obvious, but we still feel conflicted. I believe this is because Humanism shapes the modern ethic and deeply influences each one of us. Television, social media, and universities all proselytize its message, remind us of the problems in this world, and then provide a passionate answer for how we can respond.

I am more affected by Humanism than I realize. So are you. When I advocate for a social cause, I receive the emotional and practical support of society. Co-workers, classmates, and childhood friends celebrate my work.

But when I proclaim the Gospel, both here and throughout the world, I am viewed with suspicion. People perceive me as a little too religious. Some may even accuse me of doing harm by advocating foreign beliefs and disturbing the peace.

In my conversations with Christians, I see a lot more concern for social issues, but less for the Great Commission. It makes me wonder if we're allowing Humanism to shape us more than our faith. The solution is not to de-emphasize justice; if anything, we need more attention and effort. Instead, the solution is to restore the Gospel to its place of primacy and then allow everything else to flow outward.

None of this minimizes the importance of fighting injustice in our society; instead, it prioritizes the Gospel as the main solution. The people of God should be found on the front lines in exposing and addressing each one of these problems, and we must continue to uphold the grace of Jesus as the ultimate solution for mankind. Don't buy into the lie telling us we must choose between the two.

We will not redeem society through our social justice alone. Only Jesus holds that power. He teaches social justice, but the road must run through His redemption and grace. A renewed focus on the mission of God will harm our reputation but lead to lasting justice. I believe it's worth it.

A NEW PERSPECTIVE

Let's pause for a moment. It's easy to get insecure when you contemplate the mission of God. Most of us are just trying to make it in our day-to-day lives. Work stress, family tension, and financial stress sap our strength. Few Christians will live overseas. The rest of us may find it difficult to reconcile our day-to-day struggles with the reality of a lost world and its problems. I certainly relate.

It's easy to discount the theology of missions, because we struggle with the application. It's too intense to think about those who don't know Jesus, so we ignore it and focus on something more tangible. While tempting, it is not the right approach. We are in dangerous waters when we let our emotions dictate our theology.

Let's start by reprioritizing the Gospel before evaluating where it fits in our lives. We need to rediscover the power of the message along with the sobriety of our responsibility. A Humanistic worldview views this through a self-focused lens, focusing primarily on how it all fits into my life and my own dreams. A Kingdom worldview starts with God's dreams and uses that to interpret us.

Ultimately, reconciling the world is God's mission. He is the one working through us, though we play a critical role. Faithfulness is our responsibility. He will lead some of you to move overseas and serve as missionaries, but most of us will stay. When we embrace a Kingdom worldview and a commitment to sacrificial love, we'll find where we fit. But when we obsess over where we fit, we'll miss the opportunity to truly promote justice in our world.

THE HOPE FOR MANKIND

Embracing the Gospel necessarily leads to social change, but social change does not necessarily lead to the Gospel. Only Jesus truly transforms. The United States has deep racial divides, and many other countries I've visited are even worse. Ditto for economic disparity, sexual abuse, and misogyny. The problem is not our culture; the problem is our sin. Social efforts and sensitivity training may change behavior, at least to a degree. Legislation can alleviate systemic injustice. But these are temporary treatments for symptoms of the underlying disease.

Symptoms are serious. They can kill if untreated. But treating symptoms alone will always prove insufficient. The root disease is the sin within the heart of mankind, tainting whatever it touches and corrupting culture itself. Sin is the source of systemic injustice. Sin is the root of abuse. If you believe in Jesus, you hold the cure—a cure unavailable to entire cultures that are being destroyed as a result. That is injustice, so go do something about it.

We should fight racism. We should stand up for the oppressed. We should expose the darkness in our culture. The Gospel restores whatever it touches. It starts with the heart; its power then radiates out to transform culture itself. Anything less is not the full Gospel.

CHAPTER 11

CONTEXTUALIZATION: THREE PATHS

Cultural change is expanding across every part of the United States. I recently spent two months traveling across the United States to visit churches, and the tour confirmed my suspicions. Our nation is changing, and it's not limited to a particular region. Each stop revealed the same emerging tension between church and culture. It's a new world, and many believers feel confused on which path to take.

The long hours driving provided time to reflect. There's something captivating about the open road, a boundless freedom extending beyond the horizon. Each exit represents opportunity—where do you want to go? Who do you want to be? Turn left for the beach, right for the mountains, continue on for the city. I could see the turns clearly enough, but not beyond to their destination. Everything is a possibility for a brief moment, but eventually you must choose a path.

It's a metaphor for Christianity in America in our quest to navigate the future, seeking to discover which road leads to the Kingdom. I believe we stand in a moment of possibility, and believers are taking different roads. We do not always see the implications of the turns we make; it's easy to deceive ourselves into thinking we can continue to stand with a foot in both the Kingdom and the world.

Don't be fooled, there is a final destination to each path. I worry many Christians live on spiritual cruise control and simply follow the flow of traffic. History proves this an unreliable map to find God.

I cannot decisively settle the debate on how Church and culture intersect. My view of the future is limited like everyone else. But I believe in a God who leads His Church. If we allow cultural trends to steer, we will end up in the wrong location. Let's reflect on who is truly leading us in this crucial hour and wake up to the significance of our time. Our choices today will shape our future.

CONTEXTUALIZATION

All believers wrestle with the same basic question: How do we contextualize the Gospel for a modern, Humanist culture? Contextualization is not a new struggle for the Body of Christ. If you're unfamiliar with the term, it simply refers to the way we put something into context or make it fit so our culture can understand the message.

Christianity is expressed differently around the world. Each culture contextualizes the message of Jesus in significant ways. Churches look different in England than they do in India. This is both beautiful and necessary to see the Kingdom advance.

The importance of this concept was evident in the earliest days of the Church. In the Book of Acts, we read the first church council convened to discuss the thorny issue of integrating Gentile believers. Up to this point, most growth occurred amongst Jews. Once Greeks started to follow Christ, these first believers started to question which aspects of the faith were universal and which were mere reflections of Jewish culture.

The council debated the topic and reached the conclusion that "we should not make it difficult for the Gentiles who are turning to God."[46] They only required the new believers to avoid idolatry and sexual immorality as part of their new faith, but they did not ask them to adopt Jewish customs. In other words, the leaders affirmed the Gospel is meant to be contextualized to the local culture. This proved a critical factor in its global spread.

I've worked with churches around the world. In doing so, I've seen a glimpse of the mosaic of the global Body of Christ. Each culture represents aspects of God's character, and it's powerful to see these redemptive qualities within local churches. However, local believers must also wrestle with places in which the Kingdom radically differs from their cultural worldview. No nation is exempt.

Consider American Christianity. Much of what we see as quintessential church life is the way a past generation contextualized the Gospel. Jesus and His disciples never baked a potluck casserole, used puppets to teach children, or sang with an organ. They didn't have a worship band, a coffee bar, or a bumper video before a sermon. There is nothing wrong with these things, but they're also not essential to the faith. Except coffee. They're small examples of how we've contextualized the Gospel to fit our culture. If it helps people know Jesus, let's use them. If they become a hindrance, let's cut them.

Everyone contextualizes the Gospel message to some extent, but there are significant disputes regarding how far to take it. We probably all agree we should not seek to recreate a first century agrarian village. We intuitively see the need for the Gospel to fit culture. The problem is when we take it so far that it's no longer the Gospel.

Jesus' teaching challenges everyone in some way. His words are intended to make us uncomfortable. To remove this element of our faith is to remove Jesus. Paul refers to this as a stumbling block. No matter who you are, embracing the Gospel will require you to break with societal norms, and people will not like it. We should be suspicious of a Christian faith which effortlessly fits the surrounding culture.

On the flip side, our cultural practices might become an unnecessary stumbling block. Maybe someone hates casserole or has a fear of puppets. Perhaps they're introverted, and the intense social environment of a large church frightens them. Or maybe elements of typical church life reflect suburban America to such an extent that others feel left out. We should always be willing to adapt these practices to reach people.

A multi-ethnic church in an urban environment won't look like a small-town Baptist church or the fast-growing suburban trend of the last decades. Effectively reaching Humanists requires a different approach from reaching Cultural Christians.

This is the tension found in international missions. In eras past, locals who embraced Jesus were also baptized into British and American culture. This tragically suppressed the beauty of their local customs. African believers were taught to sit on their hands in worship and forced to learn English. In some countries, believers were even renamed with English names to replace those assigned at birth. Much resistance to the Gospel is more a fight against creeping Westernization than it is to the actual words of Christ.

The last half century has seen a remarkable shift in missional thinking. Most agencies now affirm the importance of new believers contextualizing the message to fit their society. In Muslim countries, believers may choose to meet on Friday rather than Sunday, and a service may involve chants more than singing. In Hindu countries, there is a greater emphasis on the reality of the spiritual world than in the knowledge-centric views of the West.

This has led to significant church growth around the world. It also forced believers to build deep foundations in the Word of God. We can only appropriately contextualize when His Word shapes us more than the surrounding culture.

Western Christianity hasn't had to grapple with this issue as much as Asian believers due to Cultural Christianity's long dominance. But times are changing and, as culture and Church diverge, we need to rediscover the essentials of our faith while also showing a willingness to discard old expressions. We need to contextualize; however, it will only work if we have strong foundations in the Kingdom worldview. If not, we'll keep adjusting to culture to such an extent that we no longer carry a message.

Though the Kingdom must be adapted to the local context, we must remember it is always counter-cultural. It's designed to fit within the beauty of culture while simultaneously transforming it from the inside-out. We lose our prophetic voice when we contextualize too much. The Kingdom is intended to change culture, to upset the status quo, and to provoke controversy. Sin destroys people and Jesus holds the cure. Refusing to address sin in order to stay relevant cheapens the message of Jesus. Let's resist the urge to sterilize the Gospel so we fit in with polite society.

Unfortunately, rightly contextualizing to culture is never easy. Most believers agree we need to adapt but do not know how. It's like driving on the highway—each path eventually leads to a different place, but it's hard to see beyond today. And it's far too easy to follow the flow of traffic without ever considering the destination.

Finding a healthy balance is difficult. This process requires genuine discernment, prayer, and study in the Word. Godly people will disagree on specific issues, and, once we reach a consensus, culture will probably change again and force us to start over. It's why Jesus gave us the Holy Spirit. It's why He is the Head of the body. Let's trust Him to lead.

As we grapple with the implications of living in a Humanist world, I want to highlight two extreme approaches to contextualization. Some believers refuse to adapt at all. They seek to restore Cultural Christianity and, with it, a past version of American history. I believe they walk the path of *denial*. On the other extreme, some people believe the Church must fully conform to culture to stay relevant. They walk a path of *surrender*, willing to yield the teachings of Jesus in order to fit within society.

Most Christians try to stay in the middle but still run into difficulties. I see many churches refusing to address sin, not because they no longer believer it's a problem, but instead because they believe it's better to build bridges of understanding before addressing the thorny issues. I understand the logic and agree in certain situations; however, I believe the words of Jesus stand on their own, and it's OK to conflict with our society. The light of Jesus draws people—not Cultural Christianity nor a church watered down to look like the world.

I see other churches preach against all cultural changes. Though we need to stand up for righteousness, we also need to ensure the Gospel remains our main focus. It's too easy to spend our best energy fighting against cultural trends, which is a losing battle and will not lead to real change. We need revival more than new legislation.

I advocate for the path of *distinction*. This approach calls us to clearly stand on our faith, including the places we disagree with the surrounding culture. Our attitude should be a mixture of resolve and humility. Distinction requires us to reject Secular Humanism and its pull on the faith. At the same time, I believe it frees us to love Humanists and find places of shared understanding without feeling the need to compromise.

Before we consider the various approaches, please recognize this chapter is not meant as ammunition for your next Facebook fight. I have good friends who fall on opposing sides of contextualization. As a result, they often wind up advocating for different approaches on specific cultural issues. We can be clear and loving. We can listen well without compromising our beliefs.

I hope a better understanding of worldview will illuminate the path we need to travel. Rather than fighting over each cultural "hot-button," let's pause for a moment and consider our overall approach to worldview change. Our core concern is to discover which road will lead us to the Kingdom, nothing else. When this is better defined, I believe it will be far easier to discern individual topics.

PATH ONE: DENIAL

I once read a Christian author who believed the bass instrument is from the devil because, heaven-forbid, it may lead to dancing. I listened to a radio interview in which a prominent evangelist encouraged a group of South American pastors to sing American hymns instead of the upbeat songs which better fit their culture. I've dealt with the fallout from people who aggressively taught that the King James Bible is the only translation authorized by God. Each example is an attempt to make a past form of church sacred. This is the path of *denial*.

Those who embrace this road do not see the need to contextualize and view any change at all as a threat to the Church. They still believe it's possible to roll back the clock and go back in time. This will not work. The 1950s are gone, and they are never coming back. If we canonize the past, we'll alienate the present. In many ways, I fear this is exactly what's happening.

I see this most clearly today among the many believers who think electing a Christian to public office alone will reverse the momentum of Humanism and restore the Church's power in our society. I believe they misdiagnose our nation. Politics merely reflect culture; a few liberal politicians suppressing Christians is not our main problem. Our greatest challenge is to live wholeheartedly for the Kingdom in the midst of a rapidly changing world. Politics cannot stop the momentum of culture change. We need revival, and that starts with revived hearts.

Political power has never proved a reliable tool to advance

the Kingdom, especially in a society that is embracing a new belief system. Winning a few elections will prove transitory at best in our quest to engage with society.

Despite my strong words, I absolutely see the need for Godly men and women serving in politics, and I pray for more. I also believe a nation built on the commands of God will thrive. My problem is with the attempt to restore the Church's power through politics. Christians in public office still serve an important role, and I will present a few ideas for how we should engage with government in the next chapter, but political power should never be our goal. The Kingdom requires an inside-out approach. We reach people with the Gospel. The power of God then transforms individuals, families, and eventually whole societies. This cannot be legislated.

I believe the majority of believers hold this perspective, perhaps to the surprise of our nonbelieving neighbors. Most Christians realize our way forward is not through politics. Apart from a few extreme views, no Christians openly advocate for some form of a theocracy.

Unfortunately, our society paints an unfair charactiture of Christians as power hungry politicos whose main concern is power. The media's laziness is partially to blame—it's easier to find an extreme voice to bump up the ratings then it is to truly learn the nuance of an opposing viewpoint—but we're also at fault for not clarifying our approach. This leaves plenty of room for misinterpretation.

Let's search our hearts and repent of any unhealthy drive for power, and then let's proactively describe a different path for the future. More than anything, let's then make sure our words line up with our actions.

Society is changing, whether we like it or not. Your church might resist the change for another decade, but eventually you'll discover yourself on an island. Jesus designed His Body to adapt. It's why the Church thrived for two thousand years and is still vibrant around the world today. We don't need to fear change, but we do need to firmly anchor to the Gospel in the midst of it.

PATH TWO: SURRENDER

Denial tries to force culture to change to fit the church. *Surrender* demands the church change to fit the culture. You see it when trendy Christians signal their allegiance to the Humanist ethic and rebuke believers for our old-fashioned beliefs.

Their message is based on the subtle belief that Humanism is morally superior. This is never said outright, but I believe the sentiment is evident in the underlying arguments. Those with this approach believe Christianity must conform to stay relevant and not lose our place in society. Any divergence between the worldviews is seen as a flaw in the Church.

We see this most clearly in instances when the Bible's teaching conflicts with society. It's often fellow Christians who present the strongest attack against the traditional practices of the faith, as though they feel guilty for being a Christian and not a better Humanist. They rarely abandon the Bible in their quest for conformity and instead invent a new line of interpretation which allows their faith to adapt to Humanism.

This is common today, especially online. I find it easy to get caught up arguing a specific issue and lose sight of the big picture. Our conflict is rarely rooted in complicated biblical interpretation; instead, the problem is based in worldview. Many Christians have adopted Humanism. Most seek to maintain their faith while allowing Humanism to guide their morality. This puts them in conflict with both the Cultural Christian and Kingdom worldviews.

The *surrender* approach prioritizes removing cultural barriers above all else. The underlying motivation is simply to fit in. It's also unsustainable. Humanism is built on an opposite premise from the Gospel. If you follow the lead of the world, you will eventually look like the world.

I believe these individuals genuinely love God and want people to thrive, but I have deep concerns about Christians and churches traveling this direction.

Historian Rodney Stark has identified this tendency as a long-term trend in American religious history.[48] Denominations start off radical with the first generation and then gradually seek to reduce tension with the surrounding culture. Initially these adjustments might be healthy and balanced. But if left unchecked, they will cause churches to lose critical elements of their faith, shedding their core beliefs until they end up with a universalist doctrine. We see this trend in many of the historic mainline denominations.

The initial concern is the future of the church. Those advocating this approach believe we must adapt the church's teaching to fit the culture to stay relevant, but it does not work. Compromise doesn't lead to growth; instead, history proves it will kill the church. Starks notes this approach always leads to a sharp decline in involvement. People turn to Jesus and the church because we offer answers to the world's brokenness; our power is because we're different. When we're no longer distinct, we have nothing left to offer.

Becoming like the world will never reach the world. The light of Jesus leads people out of the darkness, not our cultural savvy. Let's resist the urge to dim our brightness to better fit in with our neighbors. We need to contextualize and remove unnecessary stumbling blocks to reach a modern era, but we cannot surrender our faith. Let's hold the Word of God as our anchor, even when it comes at a price.

PATH THREE: DISTINCTION

Both of the previous approaches seek the same goal: to maintain social standing. The path of denial tries to re-assert the church into a place of cultural dominance. The path of surrender takes the "if you can't beat them, join them" stance. But is social standing really the goal of our faith? I understand the desire to fit in with the world around us, but I don't believe it is the right motivation.

The Kingdom is counter-cultural by design. Yes, the message of the Gospel must adapt to each environment, but it does not change. The path of distinction calls us to boldly proclaim our core message and to clarify our differences in a respectful way. This approach does not try to force the rest of the world to conform to us, but at the same time is clear that we do not intend to conform to the world.

We need to start looking beyond the two extremes. A culture war doesn't need to be a zero-sum conflict. We don't need to surrender to Humanist morality nor do we need to try to force society back into the fold of Cultural Christianity. Neither of these roads will lead to the Kingdom, but I fear many people feel they're our only options. I believe there is an altogether different path.

Let's put our primary energy into actually living the Kingdom, moving beyond words and into action. A theoretical worldview cannot transform. But if the Gospel is true, if the Holy Spirit lives inside of us, then we're free to create a new culture. This Kingdom culture is distinctly different and thus emerges as a powerful witness to a broken world.

I believe the world is increasingly dissatisfied with Humanism. Society is sticking with it because they don't see any other options. Unfortunately, the Church is the last place many people look for answers. This is often due to the flawed history of Cultural Christianity. Words alone cannot cure this problem, but our lifestyle can. We can't force someone to adapt to our standards, but we can do our part to change the narrative. This occurs primarily on a local level, because people leave changed when they genuinely touch the Kingdom.

It's OK to start small. We don't need to change culture overnight. Instead, we need substance. We need to truly, authentically live a Kingdom culture. If we do, it will change everything.

Jesus told us the Kingdom of Heaven is like a mustard seed—small, insignificant, overlooked. But healthy things grow. At first, it's just a fledgling shoot out of the ground, but one day we wake up and everything is transformed.

Let's put our best energy into creating this culture together as local churches. We're spending far too much time reacting to the latest trends and arguments in our culture and far too little time investing in healthy Kingdom life. We need a priority shift.

God empowered His Church to live the Kingdom. Sure we'll make mistakes along the way, and it'll still be difficult, but this is our calling. The world is desperate for goodness, sacrificial love, humility, and peace—all the things we've been given.

When our neighbors see the authenticity of our walk with God, some will be drawn to it while others will reject the message. It's exactly what happened to the early church. But be warned: We'll still feel like outsiders no matter how perfectly we live a Kingdom culture. In fact, the more we do so, the more tension we'll feel. That's the price to pay, but I believe it's worth it.

Distinction starts by clarifying core beliefs. I'll start with a few: We believe in a supreme and Holy God who created all things. We believe God created mankind in His own image. We believe man sinned and introduced death into the world. We believe we cannot earn our way back into God's goodness. We believe God loved us so much that He sent His only Son to die for our sins. We believe Jesus rose from the dead and promised us a new life. We believe we receive God's grace through faith alone. We believe He put His Spirit inside of us to transform us from the inside out, so we might sacrificially love and live according to God's standards. We believe we carry a responsibility to spread this message around the world.

There's more to it, that's why we have the Bible. But just these statements alone lead to a radically different worldview.

If we genuinely believe them to be true, it will place us on a different road from the world around us.

When we confidently hold to our beliefs, we're free to graciously engage with our neighbors. While we disagree on several significant issues, there are countless other places we do agree with our society. These represent opportunities to build bridges and pursue common goals. Let's fight to end cycles of poverty, let's work to educate at-risk children, let's stand against gender violence, and let's advocate for integrity and humility in politics.

Even in our disagreements, the path of distinction creates opportunities for compromise. This is the legacy of the United States. Colonial Baptists and Methodists faced immense pressure from the established churches and the more secular Deists who held power. They disagreed on core doctrine and at times were subject to physical persecution. But because of their distinct beliefs, these radical believers were able to negotiate with their opponents to find a fair solution for everyone. This represented a major global breakthrough.

Up to this point in history, religious freedom was a rare and fleeting concept, but now it's recognized as a core civil right. I hope we can continue in this legacy and build upon it to find fair solutions to maintain our freedom to worship God.

This will not take place if we live in denial or choose to surrender. Humanism may be a prominent worldview in our nation, but it's not the only one. We don't need to fight each other to gain power; instead, let's continue to build a truly free society.

CHOOSE YOUR PATH

Which path are you currently travelling? You might recognize you're a functional Humanist. If so, take a moment to prayerfully consider if this is the road you intend to travel. I believe many believers walk this path without even knowing it.

Others might realize they're still fighting to restore Cultural Christianity. If so, refocus on the message of Jesus rather than the latest cultural issue. Put Him first. Invest more time in the Word than reading blogs and online news. Take a moment to question how much of what you profess translates into action in your life.

Most believers remain undecided. Each path seems appealing in its own way. For those still living in this moment of possibility, I challenge you to build deep foundations in the Word. We cannot contextualize the Gospel to fit culture if we don't know the Gospel. The more clearly you stand on the Word of God, the more you'll see how to respond to societal changes.

The last chapter will explore how this translates into specific action. I believe it's not enough to proclaim a Kingdom; in order to be a light to the world we must live the Kingdom. Things might seem confusing, and the way forward may appear shrouded in darkness, but I believe it's quite simple. We have a choice to make: Follow the path of the world or set out on the path of the Kingdom.

We may live in that brief moment of possibility, with each option stretching out before us. Now is the time when we need to choose. I've made my decision. Let's take a step of faith, knowing it may cost us. It's the same step countless believers have taken. There's more work to be done. Now it's our turn.

CHAPTER 12

THE WAY FORWARD

Worldview is difficult to understand and even harder to change. I hope the preceding chapters helped you identify your belief system and answer the question posed in Chapter 1: What is your worldview? This was a primary reason for writing this book. Many of us feel the changes in culture and the tension in our own minds but lack language to talk about it. Simple awareness is a critical first step.

Unfortunately, awareness alone is not enough. Adding better terminology to our societal tension does not save. It's similar to a weather forecast—we may better understand what's happening, and this is important, but a forecast alone cannot tell us how to respond.

I experienced this first hand while traveling. One evening, I mindlessly scrolled my newsfeed and noticed a late-season tropical storm brewing in the Gulf. It felt irrelevant at the time. I was fifteen hundred miles away. Two days later, the storm rapidly intensified and meteorologists projected 150 mile-per-hour winds would crash ashore. The storm started to dominate the news cycle.

The projected path of the storm showed it hitting the Florida panhandle, traversing Georgia, the Carolinas, and then exiting out to sea near the Virginia border as a tropical storm. I started to pay attention because this was right where I was visiting in a motorhome. The center of the storm was forecasted a hundred miles to our south.

The forecast was important and woke me up to the reality of the situation, but it left me confused on how to respond. Do we try to escape the storm? Or would doing so put us in danger of getting stuck on the road when the winds hit? How guaranteed is the actual path? I realized there was no realistic way to escape the massive storm and felt moving put us at a greater risk. We decided to stay put and avoid the roadways. Our campsite had a secure building, and I moved my vehicle away from trees. I felt reasonably secure as we waited for the rain.

The mournful wail of a tornado siren heralded the first sign of trouble, interrupting our family dinner and forcing us into a nearby basement. My Kansas upbringing kept me confident. The warning lifted after an hour, and the weather radar showed the intensity moving away. We waited a little longer and then ventured out to the motorhome to put our kids to bed. I mistakenly thought the adventure was over.

Five minutes later a blast of wind shook the motorhome. I shared a nervous glance with my wife. Then it happened again, this time even more intense. I checked the weather again and my stomach dropped. The storm was traveling further north than predicted. The calm we experienced earlier was the center, the eye of the storm. It was passing right overhead, and now it was time for the winds.

I never thought I'd Google "how much wind does it take to knock over a motorhome," but the question felt quite relevant. For those interested, it's somewhere between sixty to eighty miles-per-hour. We appeared safe, but it was close; the storm still maintained tropical storm force strength.

An anxious hour ticked past in which I second-guessed every decision. Did I make the right call? Intense floods and tornados were ravaging the towns further away, driving there would be equally dangerous. But strong winds still shook our motorhome. I felt helpless. The parable of Jesus sleeping in the storm took on a new meaning.

It took forever until things started to calm down. The center moved further east, the rain stopped, and I finally found a few hours of sleep.

In discussing worldview, I feel like I'm forecasting the weather. I'm not sure if complete accuracy is possible. On the one hand, it's becoming increasingly clear that change is rapidly intensifying and there is no way to escape. I pray this book is like a good forecast, allowing you to better understand your world.

But no matter how accurate, a forecast does not provide a clear course of action. It's important to understand our environment, but at some point, this must translate into a response. As cultural change continues to build and intensify, I believe Christians need a plan.

The goal of this last chapter is to bridge the gap between awareness and action. I acutely feel my own inadequacy. I'm convinced the Kingdom is the only hope for this world. I'm certain neither Humanism nor Cultural Christianity will lead us into life. That much is clear. But I still wrestle with how to apply this to my everyday life.

In confusing times, we start by building upon *what we do know* before tackling *what we don't know*; otherwise, we'll spend all of our energy stuck in our conflicting emotions and swirling thoughts. I do know the Gospel alone saves, the Bible is a sure foundation, and Jesus will lead His Church. Let's start there; even if the forecast changes, these truths will provide an anchor.

As I wrap up this book, I want to end by suggesting next

steps for believers to respond to a changing world on a personal, church, city, and national level. If we want to live the Kingdom, we must translate our awareness into action. My ideas are incomplete, and I cannot see the future, but I believe this is a good start. Ultimately, I trust in the leadership of Jesus. He slept in a violent storm because He is in control of this world. Jesus is not intimidated by the changing culture. When we fail to respond perfectly, or even steer the boat into the waves, He'll be there to lead us out.

Take a risk today. Step out in faith. Put action to what you claim to believe. And, amid it all, trust in the power of Jesus to see you through it.

PERSONAL ACTION

Cultural Christianity, Humanism, and every other worldview lacks a solution to the fundamental problem of sin. This is the power of the Gospel. The grace of God empowers me to grow into who I was made to be and allows me to live in close relationship with Jesus.

I believe the single most important way we respond is by proactively growing in our walk with God. A relationship with Jesus is, well, a relationship after all. Time and investment will draw us closer. Distance will pull us apart. This relationship is what will carry us through any change in our world.

Humanism loses its appeal when we live closely connected to the person of Jesus. We need to avoid the temptation to live reactively—whether it's fighting against encroaching Humanism or entrenched Cultural Christianity. Instead, focus your best time and attention on drawing near to God. Counterfeits hold no appeal when compared to the authentic.

Does your schedule indicate your relationship with Jesus is a top priority? How much time do you spend absorbing the world's messages—social media, news, radio—compared to the time you spend alone with Him? I think re-establishing the simplicity of this relationship is the starting point for most people.

Consider taking a radical step and getting off all news and social media for a week, then spend the extra time in worship and the Word. See how you feel at the end. Every time I do this, I realize how much our world's collective anxiety is robbing me of peace. As a result, I set stronger limits on my media intake. Most of us probably need a recalibration.

Once you invest in your walk with God, then you need to turn around and sacrificially love others. Our culture has rebranded the word *love* to mean acceptance. It drives me crazy. *Love* is laying down your life, *love* is sticking with people in their darkest moments, *love* is making others great—even at your own expense. Love includes acceptance at a fundamental level, but it might also confront destructive patterns. True love doesn't accept the destruction of a friend. Acceptance is a low bar. Let's learn to love again in the way of Jesus.

Find a way to sacrifice for someone else. I'm not just talking about paying it forward. Sorry, but a three-dollar cup of coffee isn't really a sacrifice, though still a nice gesture. Instead, find a place to serve and stop worrying about how it all fits with your gifting. This doubles as marriage advice. We need to reject the contemporary trend steering us to mutual self-benefit and rediscover the power of covenantal love.

Everyone wants to be loved—not just accepted, but also truly loved. Most people just can't get over themselves enough to do it. It's not easy, but it is incredibly powerful; and this is the inheritance of those who know Jesus.

Finally, to truly live this way, you also need to prioritize finding a healthy local church. We live surrounded by a Humanist culture which is constantly growing in its intensity. You can lament reality all you want, but if you want to overcome, you need to commit to walk with other believers. This is another important starting point for many people: Stop searching for a church with a consumerist mindset; instead, find a place with people who love Jesus and genuinely want to seek the Kingdom. Then stick with it.

None of this is rocket science. The problem is that it's counter-cultural, and this is why we resist. We want immediate gratification, and we want things to revolve around us. God doesn't work that way. It's essentially the point of the whole Bible.

I'm convinced that once you experience the Kingdom, you'll never go back. The cheap, rebranded "love" of Humanism, the intensely self-centered lifestyle, the anxious desire to self-actualize, the outrage at the problems of the world will never bring us life. Only Jesus satisfies. Let's keep our attention on Him, and everything else will fall into place.

CHURCH ACTION

Cultural Christianity allowed churches to get lazy. When society is built on Christian terminology, traditions, and symbols, people will eventually pick up the core tenets of the faith. Even unbelievers knew the Bible and Christian doctrine in years past.

As a result, churches started to focus on a great Sunday morning experience to attract members. Solid teaching, engaging worship, and a good kids ministry. Throw in a guest ministry team, and you have a fast-growing church. Discipleship became an optional component rather than a chief concern.

Those days are over. I'm all for a dynamic Sunday service, but this alone will not stem the tide of Humanism. Perhaps it was also the flaw within Cultural Christianity. The Gospel is meant to be accessible for everyone, no matter how broken, but it's also designed to transform.

When service attendance is our only scoreboard, we're essentially surrendering to the world's culture. One great sermon is not enough to offset a steady bombardment of Humanist messages and a firmly ingrained belief system. I'm thankful for great preaching, but it's just a part of effective ministry. The real work is the culture we create the rest of the week.

Our approach to ministry needs to change. Churches need to prioritize creating a discipleship culture which allows people to learn to live the Kingdom together in community. Television and public schools no longer teach the Bible. I think it's a blessing in disguise to force us to do our job as parents, friends, pastors, and small group leaders.

Christians are up against a negative perception in our culture—one we earned fair and square. We lose our authority to speak truth when we live like hypocrites. The stakes are too high to surrender. We need to live like true disciples of Jesus.

Authenticity by itself is incomplete. If our lives are a mess, then being real won't get us very far without some type of change. But genuine faith and love will always prove extremely powerful. The world is desperate to find people who live at peace, are confident, and who sacrificially love others. When we create this culture in our churches, we regain the authority to stand as a prophetic voice to our world.

Churches will need to stand for righteousness. This will generally not be well received—that's the whole point of being a prophetic voice. But we need to match this with the integrity of our own lives. We need to live the change we seek if we want the authority to talk about it.

Pause for a moment and imagine the impact of churches living a Kingdom culture. Perhaps you've never experienced this. I'm deeply sorry if this is the case. I know church life can carry a lot of pain, but please don't give up. The Kingdom is worth it.

SOCIAL ACTION

I've seen many of the world's problems up close: talking with genocide survivors, hearing the stories of people who lived through chemical weapon attacks, listening to the anguish of refugees, responding to natural disasters, stepping foot into countries engulfed in civil war, meeting modern slaves, and visiting the world's worst slums. Life isn't fair, and far too many people never get a real chance to escape cycles of poverty.

Most problems are incredibly complex. The more I see the world, the more I realize how nuanced everything is and cracks form in my comfortable, black-and-white political opinions. This is why I believe Jesus is the only hope for this world.

The Humanist ethic is built on the idea of "do no harm." Social impact is often reduced to recycling, voting, and occasionally showing up to a protest or at least signaling your allegiance online if showing up is too much work. Perhaps these are a good start, but they're just baby steps.

Sacrificial love alone will change the world. Go through your history book and look at someone who sparked real change. Inevitably, you'll discover it cost them everything, and disproportionally they were strong believers. This is no accident.

If I am my chief concern, I will not make a lasting impact. Cycles of poverty do not have simple solutions, and hashtags don't help much with long-standing ethnic tensions. Governments can help fight against systemic problems, but they're far more limited than people realize.[49] The world's problems tend to originate in the heart. Anger, greed, bias, and out-of-control appetites fuel most injustice. Legislation alone will never be enough.

Enter the local church. We hold a unique opportunity to make a difference if we're willing to get involved in our communities. What if, instead of railing against society's problems, we started to serve the places of need?

A school district administrator challenged a group of pastors in my city to each adopt a local school. Government funding wasn't enough to provide the support the parents and teachers needed, but churches could bridge the gap. Though we certainly need Godly men and women in government to work on funding, we also need ordinary people willing to serve a need in the community.

Our church adopted two schools in our neighborhood and, more than a decade later, we provide mentoring in reading to every single elementary student who requests support—over 300 kids. Reading proficiency shot through the roof, catapulting these schools to among the top performing in the school district. Of course, it's the hard work of the teachers and administration who deserve the most credit, but it also demonstrates the power of churches engaging the community.

The collaboration caught the attention of the new superintendent, and we've now expanded to a partnership with over forty churches, with a goal to provide mentoring to every single student in the whole district.

When people build foundations with God, learn to love sacrificially, and serve in the context of a local church, then we possess an incredible opportunity to impact our society. Increased funding and new laws will not be enough to fix our world's problems, so it's time for the Church to engage.

We need to spend more time making a difference than we do angrily reacting to a changing culture. The world may think we're crazy, but they cannot discount us if we stand on the front lines serving where no one else is willing. It will expose the fatal flaw in Humanism. If people live to maximize self, they will not commit to lay down their lives for their neighbor. Being true to self never results in true goodness to others.

Sacrificial love provided the engine behind the early church's radical growth, and it will guarantee our relevance for years to come. I don't worry about Humanism. Time will prove its emptiness, but I am concerned that the Church will lose sight of what we do best. Let's stop reacting to a Humanist culture and focus on proactively living the Kingdom.

NATIONAL CHANGE

I've tried to avoid politics throughout this book. This is very intentional. I believe the intensity of modern political debate and the identity we find in our political allegiance is causing too many Christians to lose sight of the bigger picture. We've allowed our politics to define our faith. That's the wrong approach; instead, let's allow our faith to shape our view of everything else.

The Kingdom always begins as an internal transformation and has little to do with political power. In fact, I believe the eras in which the Church held the most power were some of the darkest moments for believers. It's the consequence of the desire for power eclipsing the Kingdom.

I'm grateful for Godly men and women in politics, but they're not the saviors of Christianity in America. We already have a Savior, and He's the only one we need. Instead, I believe the Kingdom calls every single believer to bring the Kingdom wherever they go. For some it's the neighborhood, for others it's the classroom, and for a few, it's in government buildings.

Serving in government is difficult. We should pray for our elected officials regardless of party affiliation. I believe the best way for a politician to make an impact is for them to live a Kingdom lifestyle with authentic integrity, humility, and a willingness to serve others. Then, with this foundation, they can work for righteousness. Godly people will at times disagree on the best way to care for the poor, the role of government, and how to write fair legislation. If we work from a desire for genuine service rather than thinly veiled ambition, we'll be able to find healthy compromises. In the process, we'll also provide a powerful example to a fractured nation.

On a local level, we need Christians to step into places of service. Rather than spending our time reacting to the latest problem in Washington, let's instead seek to make a grassroots impact. Serve on a city board or commission, volunteer at a local school. Do the hard, thankless work behind the scenes. We gain influence when we make a difference far more than when we win an election. Our goal is not some sneaky attempt to establish a theocracy, but rather to seek the welfare of our community and model the love of God. If we excel in this, then we'll find far more influence—not because of political power but instead because of our example.

I'm going to stay out of policy entirely, except for one point. The Church is moving into minority status in the United States, and I believe this requires a shift in focus. In fact, I'd feel the same way even if we still held more political power. I propose Christians focus on promoting religious liberty and avoid the temptation to fight to hold power for the sake of holding power.

Legislation will not restore Christianity back into the dominant ethic of our nation. We need to learn to be the Church and to truly live the Kingdom. It's a far longer process, but it will lead to far greater results than winning the occasional election. The Church has thrived under far more hostile governments than anything we've ever seen or are likely to ever see. Politics certainly matter, and the laws of the State hold tremendous power to help or harm, but believers need to shift priorities and stop using national politics as an excuse to avoid our personal and local responsibilities.

We don't need government to support us, but it is more difficult when we're actively opposed. Religious liberty does create an environment for the Church to thrive. I believe we should all be worried by any government attempts to legislate or enforce a belief system. This is my concern with Humanism. I think it is emerging as the de facto State religion and fear attempts to impose the belief system onto religious groups. Many Humanists don't realize they live within such a strong worldview. I don't think they hold malicious intent toward believers, but instead are genuinely unaware of what they're doing. Either way, I worry they're starting to cross this line.

We should not try to force our beliefs on Humanists via the power of the State, but neither should they do the same to us. Both sides are guilty of attempting to do just that. I don't need the government to support me in preaching the Gospel, but I also don't want the government pressuring me to convert to Humanism.

I admit it can be tricky to work this out. I encourage Christians in government to find solutions and fair ways to bridge this gap as we settle into life as religious minorities in the coming decades. This was the founding legacy of our nation, and I think it still holds a wonderful example for our time.

Regardless of what happens, external pressure never dictates the future of the Church. If we live the Kingdom, we'll thrive no matter how much opposition we face. I believe we should advocate for religious liberty wherever possible, but ultimately my hope is in a God who leads His people no matter the obstacles.

Personal transformation will lead to sacrificial love and service, which will then lead to vibrant local churches. Healthy churches will create disciples in every sphere of society and impact their communities in a profound way. To the extent this becomes a reality is the extent to which we see our nation transformed. Let's get back to the basics, and let's live the Kingdom. It's an inside-out approach, and it's the only way to see a lasting change.

THE PRIMACY OF THE GOSPEL

Understanding worldview is difficult and complex. By contrast, the power of the Gospel is in its simplicity. A Humanist might emphasize the truth of a God who uniquely created us and loves us. A Cultural Christian might emphasize the truth that our sin separates us from God and leads to destruction. Both end up missing grace.

You are loved by God, and you struggle with sin. This is the fate of all humanity. Jesus entered our world to set us free and restore us back to relationship with God.

Cultural Christianity teaches us to cover up our sin. Humanism teaches us there is no sin. But only Jesus takes away our sin. That's the power of grace. Which gospel defines your life? Is it the gospel according to culture? Or the Gospel of grace?

Let's restore the power and simplicity of the Gospel, the anchor of our lives. Regardless of how complex our world becomes, and no matter the intensity of the latest cultural arguments, we can always fall back on the core message of Jesus.

When He shapes our worldview, everything else will make sense. As we learn to live accordingly, we'll wake up one day to discover the more we sacrificially love others, the more life we find for ourselves. The Humanist emphasis on self is empty and powerless to bring about any lasting change. I don't need to react against it, but I also must not get swallowed up by it. Let's be the Church; let's live the Kingdom; let's learn to sacrificially love.

The words of Jesus will outlast any cultural trend. His message is radical, and His message alone will save. "Whoever wants to save their life will lose it, but whoever loses their life for me will find it."[50]

REFERENCES

[1] Very similar to the idea of "Social Imagination" described by Charles Taylor, *A Secular Age* (Cambridge, MA: Harvard University Press, 2007), 171; and the concept of "Plausibility Structures" as taught by Peter Berger, *The Sacred Canopy – Elements of a Sociological Theory of Religion* (Garden City, NY: Doubleday, 1967). See also the Introduction to Craig Gay, *The Way of the (Modern) World: Or, Why It's Tempting to Live As If God Doesn't Exist* (Grand Rapids, MI: Wm. B. Eerdmans Publishing Co., 1998).

[2] Philip Bump, "The psychology of political beliefs (or, why hard data isn't always convincing)," The Washington Post, November 17, 2015. https://www.washingtonpost.com/news/the-fix/wp/2015/11/26/why-you-cant-convince-your-uncle-hes-wrong-about-politics/?noredirect=on&utm_term=.f18189ba3477 For additional research: Peter H. Ditto, Brittany S. Liu, Cory J. Clark, Sean P. Wojcik, Eric E. Chen, Rebecca H. Grady, Jared B. Celniker, and Joanne F. Zinger, "At Least Bias Is Bipartisan: A Meta-Analytic Comparison of Partisan Bias in Liberals and Conservatives," Perspectives on Psychological Science, January 19, 2018. http://sites.uci.edu/peterdittolab/files/2018/06/Ditto-et-al.-2018-At-Least-Bias-is-Bipartisan-A-Meta-Analytic-Comparison-of-Partisan-Bias-in-Liberals-Conservatives.pdf

[3] For example: Luke 10:25-37 and Luke 15:11-32.

[4] 2 Corinthians 10:10.

[5] Billy Fincher, *The Acts of Paul and Thecla* (Lost Books Book 13) (Scotts Valley, CA: CreateSpace Independent Publishing Platform, March 31, 2016).

6 See the Pew Research data in Chapter 2 of this book. See also Malcom Gladwell, *The Tipping Point* (Boston, MA, Little, Brown and Company, 2000) for more on "sudden" cultural changes.

7 These are obvious generalities. Geography, education, and family of origin all affect this significantly.

8 Hebrew 11:13; 1 Peter 2:11.

9 I'm specifically referring to the pluralism implicit in the concept of religious freedom. See Lesslie Newbigin, in *The Gospel in a Pluralist Society* (Grand Rapids, MI, W.B. Eerdmans, 1989) for a more in-depth treatment on this topic, including a discussion on to what extent this is even possible.

10 "America's Changing Religious Landscape," Pew Research Center, May 12, 2015. http://www.pewforum.org/2015/05/12/americas-changing-religious-landscape/

11 Ed Stetzer, "The State of the Church In America: Hint: It's Not Dying," *Christianity Today*, October 1, 2013. https://www.christianitytoday.com/edstetzer/2013/october/state-of-american-church.html

12 See Jayber Crow and Hannah Coulter.

13 See Eric Metaxas, *7 Men: And the Secret of Their Greatness* (Nashville: Thomas Nelson, 2016), 31-56 for more on William Wilberforce.

14 Greg M. Epstein, *Good Without God: What a Billion Nonreligious People Do Believe* (New York: William Morrow, 2010).

15 Matthew 22:37-39.

16 Becka Alper and Aleksandra Sandstrom, "If the U.S. had 100 people: Charting Americans' religious affiliations," Pew Research Center, November 4, 2016. http://www.pewresearch.org/fact-tank/2016/11/14/if-the-u-s-had-100-people-charting-americans-religious-affiliations/

[17] "How We Got Here: Spiritual and Political Profiles of America" Barna Research: Faith & Christianity, May 23, 2017. https://www.barna.com/research/got-spiritual-political-profiles-america/

[18] James Davison Hunter, "'America's Fourth Faith': A Sociological Perspective on Secular Humanism," *This World 19*, Fall 1987, 103-4, cited in Gay, "The Way of the (Modern) World," 203.

[19] See Patrick Deneen, *Why Liberalism Failed* (New Haven, CT: Yale University Press, 2018) for a more in-depth treatment of this topic.

[20] Taylor, *A Secular Age*, 94.

[21] Rodney Stark, *The Triumph of Christianity: How a Forbidden Religion Swept the World* (New York: HarperOne, 2001), 284-287 and Rodney Stark, *The Victory of Reason: How Christianity Led to Freedom, Capitalism, and Western Success* (New York: Random House, 2006), ix-xiii.

[22] Jeremiah 5:7-8a.

[23] Jean Twenge, "Time Period and Birth Cohort Differences in Depressive Symptoms in the U.S., 1982–2013," *Social Indicators Research Journal*, April 2015, Volume 121, Issue 2, 437–454. https://doi.org/10.1007/s11205-014-0647-1.

[24] Elinor Polack, "Research Puts Spotlight on the Impact of Loneliness in the U.S. and Potential Root Causes," *Cigna*, May 1, 2018. https://www.cigna.com/newsroom/news-releases/2018/new-cigna-study-reveals-loneliness-at-epidemic-levels-in-america

[25] Ben Kaplan, "For transplant patient Dwight Kroening, running is defined by heart," *The National Post*, November 15, 2011. http://www.nationalpost.com/transplant+patient+dwight+kroening+running+defined+heart/5715353/story.html

[26] Stark, *The Triumph of Christianity*, 273-282.

[27] Taylor, *A Secular Age*, 429.

[28] Taylor, *A Secular Age*, 245, 573.

[29] James Franklin, "The Renaissance Myth" *Quadrant* 26 (11), November 1982, 51-60. http://web.maths.unsw.edu.au/~jim/renaissance.html

[30] Stark, *The Triumph of Christianity*, 239-240.

[31] Stark, *The Triumph of Christianity*, 252.

[32] See Robert Woodberry, "The Missionary Roots of Liberal Democracy," *American Political Science Review 106*, May 2012, 244-274 for a thorough analysis of the Protestant impact on factors such as education and social reform which influenced the development of stable democracies around the world. See also Os Guinness, *Renaissance: The Power of the Gospel However Dark the Times* (Westmont, IL: IVP Books, 2014), 67-70.

[33] Gay, *The Way of the (Modern) World*, 26.

[34] Os Guinness, *The Last Christian on Earth* (Raleigh, NC: Regal House Publishing, 2010), 11.

[35] Dan Piepenbring, "Chick-Fil-A's Creepy Infiltration of New York City" *The New Yorker*, April 13, 2018. https://www.newyorker.com/culture/annals-of-gastronomy/chick-fil-as-creepy-infiltration-of-new-york-city

[36] George Yancey, "Has Society Grown More Hostile Towards Conservative Christians? Evidence from ANES Surveys," Review of Religious Research, March 2018, Volume 60, Issue 1, 71–94. https://doi.org/10.1007/s13644-017-0303-8

[37] Jonathan Haidt and Greg Lukianoff, "Why It's a Bad Idea to Tell Students Words Are Violence," The Atlantic, July 18, 2017. https://www.theatlantic.com/education/archive/2017/07/why-its-a-bad-idea-to-tell-students-words-are-violence/533970/

[38] George Yancey, *Compromising Scholarship: Religious and Political Bias in American Higher Education* (Waco, TX: Baylor University Press, 2017), 20-21, 129-134, 181-83

[39] 1 Corinthians 13:25,31-32.

[40] Peter Schjeldahl, "Dutch Master: The art forger who became a national hero," *The New Yorker*, October 17, 2008. https://www.newyorker.com/magazine/2008/10/27/dutch-master

[41] Edward Dolnick, *The Forger's Spell: A True Story of Vermeer, Nazis, and the Greatest Art Hoax of the Twentieth Century.* (New York: Harper Perennial, 2008), cited in Daniel Stashower, "Master Swindler," *The Washington Post*, July 20, 2008. http://www.washingtonpost.com/wp-dyn/content/article/2008/07/17/AR2008071702348.html

[42] Gay, *The Way of the (Modern) World*, 272.

[43] Romans 9:1-3.

[44] Joshua Packard, "Meet the 'Dones,'" *Christianity Today*, 2015. https://www.christianitytoday.com/pastors/2015/summer-2015/meet-dones.html

[45] John 8:12.

[46] Acts 15:19-21.

[47] 1 Corinthians 1:23.

[48] Stark, *The Churching of America*, 275.

[49] See Deneen, *Why Liberalism Failed and Gay, The Way of the (Modern) World*, Chapter 1 for a more detailed discussion on the role of government in modern society.

[50] Matthew 16:25.